Rosalie M. Young and Harriet H. Savage, educational therapists and specialists in learning disabilities, are associated in private practice. They have extensive experience working with youngsters from preschool through college age and have given numerous workshops and courses to parents and teachers. In Westchester County, New York, they have trained over a thousand volunteers to help children with learning disabilities.

BETTER LEARNING

How to Help Students of All Ages
Overcome Learning Problems
and Learning Disabilities

Rosalie M. Young and Harriet H. Savage
Illustrated by Judith Bahssin

A SPECTRUM BOOK

PRENTICE-HALL, INC.
Englewood Cliffs, New Jersey 07632

Library of Congress Cataloging in Publication Data

Young, Rosalie M.
    Better learning.

    "A Spectrum Book."
    Bibliography: p.
    Includes index.
    1. Learning disabilities. 2. Remedial
teaching. I. Savage, Harriet H. II. Title.
LC4704.Y68   371.92   81-19227
                            AACR2

ISBN 0-13-074609-6

ISBN 0-13-074591-X {PBK.}

This Spectrum Book is available to businesses and organizations at a special discount when ordered in large quantities. For information, contact Prentice-Hall, Inc., General Publishing Division, Special Sales, Englewood Cliffs, N.J. 07632.

© 1982 by Rosalie M. Young and Harriet H. Savage.

A SPECTRUM BOOK

The symbol discrimination and sequencing illustration on page 43 and the letter tracking illustration on page 44 are reproduced by courtesy of Ann Arbor Publishers, Inc.

10   9   8   7   6   5   4   3   2   1

Printed in the United States of America

Editorial/production supervision and interior design by Frank Moorman
Page layout by Maria Carella
Cover design by Judith Kazdym Leeds
Manufacturing buyer: Cathie Lenard

Prentice-Hall International, Inc., *London*
Prentice-Hall of Australia Pty. Limited, *Sydney*
Prentice-Hall of Canada, Ltd., *Toronto*
Prentice-Hall of India Private Limited, *New Delhi*
Prentice-Hall of Japan, Inc., *Tokyo*
Prentice-Hall of Southeast Asia Pte. Ltd., *Singapore*
Whitehall Books Limited, *Wellington, New Zealand*

CONTENTS

v

FOREWORD

How I could have used this book years ago! It would have given me an understanding of specific learning problems and would have taught me how to help my children.

When one of my daughters, a whiz at math, could not learn to read, the reading teacher at her school thought that she was emotionally blocked and recommended a psychiatrist. I complied with her request, though instinctively I knew this was not the answer. The psychiatrist agreed. After much searching and consulting with different educators, I was referred to Rosalie Young, an educational therapist. She helped my child and later my other children who had minor learning problems.

Recently, my grandson's kindergarten teacher announced that he was not ready for first grade—he had trouble rhyming; he could not hear the differences between the sounds of letters; he could not order the alphabet. In addition, he had a very short attention span. I was almost certain that he was somewhat dyslexic, and my daughter and I knew he needed help. Because of our successful past experience, we turned to Mrs. Young to evaluate the little boy, and Harriet Savage is now tutoring him. Moreover, we found that his school, like many others today, is aware of learning disabilities and offers classroom help and extra services to the children in need.

It's easy for me to sympathize with all youngsters struggling in school, because I also had similar problems. Early on, it became apparent that learning problems can be a familial trait. My children, in fact, had two strikes against them. Their learning problems are inherited not only from me, but also from my husband's family, where learning disabilities have repeatedly surfaced among close and distant relatives.

Happily, my children and grandchild have benefitted from supportive competent teaching. Not only did they learn, but over a period of time, I gained an understanding of learning problems and acquired practical ways of dealing with them.

Better Learning reflects what has taken me years to learn. If only I could have turned to an informative book like this, it would have made such a difference. From my experience I feel that *Better Learning* will be invaluable for everyone concerned with teaching children and adults.

Mary G. Rockefeller

PREFACE

This book is for everyone who desires to help a child or adult learn—parents, teachers, volunteers, therapists. Major areas of learning are covered. Although we stress the therapeutic role in teaching, the focus is on practical techniques that can be used to overcome difficulties.

We feel strongly that the academic demands made on children should not exceed their capabilities. Therefore, we present developmental timetables for the average child and school expectations at different grade levels. By using these as a reference, parents, professionals, or volunteers can measure the performance of a child and determine the level at which to start teaching. We discuss differences in the development of learning abilities and show what types and degrees of variation result in specific learning disabilities.

Much of the material in this book comes from a number of courses we have given on learning disabilities and from our years of experience in working with children and adults. We have worked with all the children, adolescents, adults, and parents described in this book. The names have been changed.

ACKNOWLEDGMENTS

This book would not have been possible without the help of our friend Edith S. Engel, an editor and freelance writer. She was the one who suggested that the material from our course and our experiences should be presented in a book. Our special thanks go to her for everything: for critically reading our manuscript, for sharing her expertise and helping us to edit. Also, we are grateful to Edith for giving us so much of her valuable time.

In addition, we want to express our appreciation to our friend and colleague, Nancy B. Katzman, a learning disabilities specialist, for her material which was the basis of the chapter on mathematics. Her knowledge of the techniques used to teach math was an important contribution to this book.

Particular thanks to our neighbor, Ethel M. McGrath, who typed our manuscript quickly, carefully, and diligently.

BETTER LEARNING

To our families
and to the children
who helped us learn

1 YOU CAN HELP AT ANY AGE

Who are the children whose school life may be a struggle from the first grade on? How can we recognize which children have specific learning disabilities? Of course, we know that some children are just slow starters and that not every child who has some difficulty in learning necessarily has a learning disability. We also realize that many thwarted adults who have difficulty coping may have had undetected learning disabilities as children. Both children and adults can be helped.

The sooner learning difficulties are spotted, however, the easier it is for the child and teacher. Much struggling and agony for both child and family can be prevented before they experience frustration and failure.

It is never too early to help any child with any type of problem. It must be remembered that the average child also occasionally needs help. Early assistance gives him or her a better chance to overcome difficulties and to progress satisfactorily. In addition, it averts the development of a poor self-image and fear of failure.

Lenny was fortunate. In kindergarten, his teachers suspected problems. As a result, he was given a complete diagnostic evaluation and consequently was tutored individually. The educational therapist who taught him worked closely with his parents and the school.

An overweight little boy with shiny black eyes, Lenny was a lovable child. Attending a kindergarten class that introduced pre-reading and writing skills, he was unable to keep up with his classmates in work or play.

It was learned that Lenny had been a high-risk baby born with an open heart valve. He recovered to be a healthy infant and an easy child whose developmental milestones were reported to be normal. Born in Spain, his parents had been educated in this country. They both worked, and the boy was always cared for by a doting grandmother who spoke only Spanish. Most of the time she dressed Lenny, even tying his shoelaces. Constantly worried about accidents, she kept him at home, rarely allowing him to play outdoors with the neighborhood children.

Lenny was never exposed to the usual pre-kindergarten experiences. His teacher reported that he had never used a crayon, pencil, or pair of scissors before entering school. She also stated that he was easily distracted and had difficulty following directions. At times, he seemed confused about what was going on in the classroom and on the playground. When hearing tests indicated no auditory problems, the school psychologist wondered about his comprehension of English and his concept development.

Testing revealed that Lenny's receptive language was average for his age. He indicated comprehension of abstract words such as *horror* and *construction* and understood place prepositions, such as *around, above, below*. For the most part his arithmetic was adequate for a five-year-old. He could touch count to thirteen and knew that five plus one more make six. His visual memory was fair and he could remember some sight words. For meaningful material his auditory memory was very good and he had a better than average fund of information. His spoken language was only slightly immature.

Yet Lenny's learning profile was uneven. His rote memory was only at a three-year-old level; he could not recite the alphabet; he could not discriminate letter sounds, but he could rhyme. From memory, the only letters he could write were A, B, and C.

Persistent when faced with difficulty, Lenny almost tried too hard. He pressured himself to please his parents, who were constantly working with him at home to improve his skills. Socially, he acted maturely for his age with adults, but his behavior with his peers was that of a much younger child.

Was Lenny ready to learn basic skills? If his difficulties stemmed solely from slow maturation, he should have been allowed to develop at his own pace and not pushed to perform beyond his capacity. On the other hand, his problems could have resulted from other factors—a bilingual home with the emphasis on a foreign language, lack of customary preschool experiences, overprotection, or a possible constitutional weakness due to having been a high-risk baby.

There was no question that the first priority was to alter Lenny's home environment through parent education. Then, after an analysis of how well the boy responded to the examiner's trial teaching, individual tutoring out of school was recommended. Lenny indicated that he was an intelligent, motivated boy.

Lenny's tutor conferred frequently with his parents as soon as she started working with him in the spring of his kindergarten year. Since Lenny seemed so pressured, she advised them to cease the home-coaching of school work. Moreover, she stressed the importance of allowing Lenny to be more independent. This meant that the parents had to impress upon his adoring grandmother that Lenny was a big boy now. He should, whenever possible, do much for himself and should be allowed more freedom to play away from his own home.

During the three months he was tutored he worked industriously to improve basic readiness skills. These included learning how to follow directions, to copy pegboard designs for spatial orientation, to write his numbers from 1 to 10, to discriminate the sounds of half the consonants and write them, and to say the alphabet. He also began to pick up sight words by recognizing their shapes and the beginning letter sounds. Furthermore, his tutor spent time talking about classroom activities and explaining different playground games. For example, one of his problems in playing kickball was his tendency to run to the wrong base. His tutor drew a chalk diagram of a diamond on the floor and rehearsed the proper way to move around the bases.

At the end of the school year his mother observed the tutoring sessions so that she could continue the work with him over the summer. In the fall, Lenny was tested at school and promoted to first grade. Recent reports indicate he is holding his own.

Problems vary with each child, and we feel that it is essential to evaluate and consider all contributing factors before deciding what sort of help is needed. In our experience, the label "learning disability" too often has been used indiscriminately and incorrectly. A good diagnosis is of the utmost importance.

Although there is general agreement that the early years are the most important for learning, it is never too late to learn. Today a person can benefit from education throughout his life, and people of all ages can be helped to overcome many learning disabilities. Roger is an illustration of how ideas about learning and relearning are changing.

Several years ago, Roger, a man of thirty-six, met Lee at a meeting of Parents Without Partners. Lee was a lawyer who had an excellent scholastic record through school and college and had become successful in her field. In contrast, Roger, a salesman, accomplished little in school. Furthermore, he had the misfortune to be the son of overcritical parents who made him feel stupid. Actually, Roger was far from stupid. He was quickwitted, full of creative ideas, and expressed himself well in conversation. Lee surmised that he was extremely intelligent and creative. One day, receiving a letter from Roger, she was horrified by his atrocious spelling and poor grammar. In addition, she could barely decipher his handwriting.

Roger was dissatisfied with his job, but aware that he could not cope with an administrative or managerial position. He could not write a business letter or organize a salesman's business report for dictation.

Lee became interested in Roger and felt impelled to help him. She remembered having seen newspaper publicity on learning disabilities and bought some books on the subject. Subsequently she began to suspect that Roger had undetected learning problems in his childhood. She initiated an evaluation and the results proved that she was correct.

Testing indicated that Roger lacked many basic skills and as he matured, his gaps had widened, causing him frustration with emotional overtones. Trial teaching showed that he learned quickly when he grasped directions. Highly motivated to learn, Roger felt that he was capable of promotion in his firm once he conquered most of his problems. He welcomed remedial help and used his lunch hours for lessons and some nights for studying. Relating readily to his tutor, he enjoyed the teaching sessions. After a year and a half of drill in spelling, grammar, composing business letters, outlining reports for his job, writing summaries of high interest stories, and so on, his basic abilities strengthened and he felt generally better about himself. With Lee's encouragement, he was ready to be on his own. All his remedial work paid off, and after a period of time, he obtained a managerial position in a good firm.

The big plus for older students and adults can be their self-motivation and realistic attitude. Roger put it in a nutshell when he wrote:

> *The lack of basic skills can leave you in a disadvantaged position. You cannot compete and rise to your full potential. To combat this lack you have to improve your basic abilities. You have to go to school or study hard on your own.*
>
> *Most people are as good as they want to be provided that they are willing to work hard toward their goal.*

Although Roger could finally be considered a success story, he had experienced many years of frustration and many periods of failure. Had his learning disabilities been detected and remediated when he was a young child, he would have avoided many problems as he grew older.

Like Lenny and Roger, there are many boys and girls, men and women, ranging in age from early childhood into adulthood, who have learning problems, and can be helped. This book gives an understanding of some learning problems and provides methods of remediation. It describes appropriate techniques for overcoming learning difficulties at different age levels in many school subjects. Just as there is no one patent medicine to cure all sicknesses, there is no one approach to overcome all learning problems. Remedial techniques must be eclectic.

Our intent is to make this book useful to all those who wish to help a child or an adult learn. Everyone can assist, not only teachers and teachers' aides, but parents, grandparents, tutors, and volunteers. In addition, countless people who work with students and adults, including social workers, librarians, mental health workers, parole officers, and therapists of all types can refer to this book for guidance.

An intelligent adolescent or adult who has had difficulty coping in and out of school may suspect that he had undetected learning disabilities as a child. A positive answer to several of the following questions may indicate that an individual had specific learning disabilities in the early years:

Does he recall writing 52 for 25? Is he still reversing numbers or letters fairly frequently?

Does he recall difficulty in remembering arithmetic facts? Is he still having trouble remembering important telephone numbers or his Social Security number?

Does he recall having trouble with different meanings of words? Is he thinking of only one definition when he hears a word, such as *file*?

Does he remember having trouble with spelling and with writing compositions? Is he still having trouble expressing his thoughts coherently? Is letter writing still a chore?

Does he recall having trouble completing reading assignments in school on time? Is he still finding reading business reports an arduous task—especially when confronted with new words?

Better Learning will give the adolescent and adult practical techniques and strategies for *self*-help if his learning problems are not too complex.

Even though children develop at different rates, there are developmental timetables for the so-called average child. In order to present them in a meaningful way, we have approximated how a child is expected to perform at different *ages*. The developmental timetables in this book are based on our use of standardized tests and our teaching experiences over a long period of time.

These timetables should help parents and teachers assess a child's development and know at what point to start teaching. To avoid frustration and failure it is crucial to start instructing a child at the level where he can succeed, and gradually proceed until step by step he has mastered all the skills that go into a particular subject.

Keeping in mind that children have different developmental timetables, those helping must also be aware of academic expectations. Therefore, we discuss and estimate how a child is expected to perform at different *grade levels*.

In teaching a child one must judge if school expectations or demands are beyond his capacity. Perhaps the school can modify demands; perhaps tutoring in and out of school will help; perhaps a different type of school is needed.

2 UNDERSTANDING LEARNING PROBLEMS AND DISABILITIES

WHAT ARE LEARNING PROBLEMS?

How we learn depends on our development in all areas. None of us develops evenly. We all have our strengths and weaknesses. If we look at our past, we each probably had a school subject that was difficult for us. Most average students have some problems in school learning. It is rare that anyone covers himself or herself with glory in every subject.

However, children with extreme differences in their abilities are the children with learning disabilities. They confuse parents and teachers when they get, for instance, A's in science and math and D's in English and social studies. It is hard to understand why so many of these children who have average or above average I.Q. (Intelligence Quotient) do so poorly in some school subjects.

What does an I.Q. really mean? An I.Q. is the total score received on a standardized intelligence test that measures ability levels.[1] For example, if a seven-year-old's performance is at a ten-year-old level, we say that he has a high I.Q. If he scores like a five-year-old, he has a low I.Q., and if he functions just as a seven-year-old should, he has an average or slightly above average I.Q. Of course, an intelligence test does not assess the social or emotional qualities so essential for learning and everyday living. In addition, it does not measure creative or artistic abilities.

[1]Individual I.Q. tests may be given in clinics, schools, agencies or private practice by trained professionals. Many schools give group I.Q. tests but these are not as reliable as individual tests. On group tests, children who cannot concentrate, cannot follow directions, or cannot read well are penalized.

The chart on page 8 should help you see how the learning-disabled child has a profile of peaks and valleys compared with the more even graph of other children. There are many factors that influence test scores, such as illness the day of the test, emotional disturbances, and anxiety. Some children and adults are just poor test-takers; their scores do not reflect their abilities. Inadequate teaching and an underprivileged background can also contribute to low achievement on the test. Thus, for many reasons an I.Q. score should not be considered a sacred statistic; I.Q. scores can be raised by improving environmental conditions, by good remediation, and by a change in emotional outlook. Nevertheless, an intelligence test is an excellent device for gaining insight into areas of strengths and weaknesses and for spotting learning problems.

It must be understood that current I.Q. tests are culturally biased and not a fair appraisal of those coming from a foreign or deprived environment. Researchers have found that constructing a culture-free test is almost impossible. New evaluation techniques for these children attempt to assess their current level of functioning. An assessment of this type, for example, SOMPA, Systems of Multicultural Pluralities Assessment, includes the measurement of thinking skills as well as social behavior at home, at school, and with peers. It also estimates learning potential which may be concealed by physical handicaps and cultural factors.

In Israel, there has been a particular problem for many years in assessing the potential of deprived children who come from cultural backgrounds as disparate as Yemen and Morocco. Dr. Reuven Feuerstein, Director of the Youth Aliyah Research Institute of Israel and professor of psychology at Tel Aviv University, has originated a Learning Potential Assessment Device which allows the examiner to encourage reactions and understanding. In addition, he has carefully designed programs with classroom material to stimulate thinking and to teach children how to reason and solve problems. Dr. Feuerstein feels strongly that mental functioning can be raised by his techniques when used by teachers who believe that a child can achieve.

Dr. Feuerstein has lectured and given courses in many universities in the United States, including Vanderbilt, Columbia, and Yale. His techniques are being tried by various educators. Research statistics are being compiled, and the results could be promising.[2]

It is evident that in some abilities the learning-disabled person may be in the superior or very superior range. In others, he is average or just below average. Needless to say, his total I.Q. score—which would be the average of his abilities—does not give a true picture of his capabilities. We have to look at the range of his strengths and weaknesses.

If a child appears to be a slow learner, it is advisable for him to have a

[2]Dr. Feuerstein has written two recent books describing his theories: *The Dynamic Assessment of Retarded Performers* and *Instrumental Enrichment*, University Park Press, Baltimore.

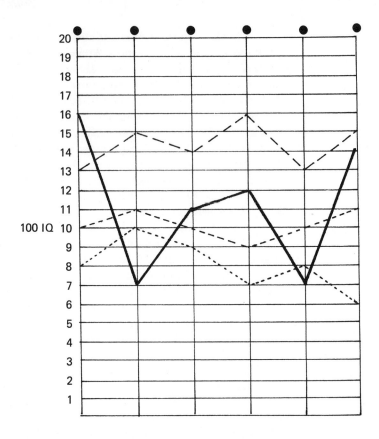

An I.Q. test is composed of numerous subtests that measure different abilities, such as arithmetic, vocabulary, reasoning, copying designs, and so on. If the highest score on each test is 20 and a child has a score of 10, he or she is right in the middle. She has an average ability for her age on that particular test. If all her tests average 10, the child's I.Q. score is 100.

The circles at the top represent different abilities tested on an intelligence test.

- - - - - This line represents the graph of the so-called average child, whose abilities vary slightly, but whose level hovers around the 10 level.

. . . . . This line represents the retarded child whose abilities range far below the 10 level.

— — — This line represents the very bright and superior child whose abilities cluster around a level well above 10.

_____ This line represents the child whose graph is a series of peaks and valleys, indicating a range of strengths and weaknesses. The pattern is not unusual for a child with learning disabilities.

thorough testing. It is important to know if his troubles stem from an over-all delay in maturation or from a real learning dysfunction.

The question is, Why does a child have such differences in abilities? Differences come from uneven development. Basically, he or she has grown more slowly in some areas than in others, for many reasons. Sometimes the cause can be traced to premature birth, physical illness, accidents, emotional disturbance, varying degrees of brain damage, or a deprived environment. Specific learning disabilities often run in families. Just as certain talents turn up, so do certain weaknesses. Learning disabilities cut across all economic and social classes; however, children from deprived environments are particularly vulnerable.

Whatever the cause, many of these youngsters and adults who have specific disabilities can overcome their weaknesses or compensate for them. They can learn with appropriate teaching. Everyone knows that Thomas Edison, Woodrow Wilson, and Albert Einstein had learning problems. Thomas Edison was considered a dunce in school and never learned to spell. Woodrow Wilson finally recognized his letters when he was nine years old, and was eleven when he learned to read. Albert Einstein began to talk at the age of four and acquired the ability to read when he was nine. These are only a few famous people who have had severe learning disabilities.

Many bright children may have difficulties when it comes to learning how to speak, listen, read, write, and do arithmetic. Some are weak in just one area. Others have a combination of problems. Patterns and degrees of difficulties vary.

Most educators feel that specific learning problems are neurologically based. But investigators have had difficulty in finding specific brain changes associated with learning problems. Now researchers are using computerized brain mapping to discover whether the brain waves of children with specific learning disabilities, sometimes called dyslexia,[3] show a different pattern from those of other children. The physiology and chemistry of the brain is the subject of world-wide research. Future study could shed light on physical, emotional, and learning problems.

HOW CAN PROBLEMS VARY?

Just as average children differ in their learning abilities, so do children with problems. But their differences are more extreme. As we mentioned before, there are many types and degrees of learning difficulties. The

---

[3]Strictly speaking, a dyslexic person is one who has difficulty in learning to read. There is no one accepted definition of dyslexia. Currently, dyslexia is a term which covers all areas of language problems—reading, writing, and spelling. Some professionals, however, use the word as an umbrella term which includes perceptual, conceptual, and behavioral problems as well as language dysfunction.

following illustrations show the performances of so-called average and above-average children and those of children with learning disabilities in different areas.

BODY IMAGE

An awareness of one's own body and the relationship of the body parts to each other and to the outside world.

An average or bright five-year-old can assemble a cut-up doll.

A five-year-old developing at a slower-than-normal rate might reverse the arms on this doll and might be slow in putting the legs in the proper place.

A five-and-a-half-year-old child showing a definite maturational lag might put the arms at the waist and the legs on the wrong side. He or she would be operating on a four-year-old level.

An older child diagnosed as brain-damaged might show no integration in assembling this doll. He might put the head at the bottom, the body on top, one arm up, the other arm down, the legs on the wrong side. He or she would be operating on a three-year-old level.

SPATIAL RELATIONS

Understanding the positions of two or more objects in relation to oneself and in relation to each other.

An average or above-average five-and-a-half to six-year-old can select the right chair for each of the three bears.

A five- or six-year-old with varying difficulties might make several mistakes. He might put the father bear in the baby's chair and the baby bear in the mother's chair.

A nine-year-old youngster who continues to have trouble with spatial relations might have trouble spacing his words and staying within the margins when writing. The following is an example of Peter's handwriting. Notice how he spilled over in writing skateboarding *and* violence.

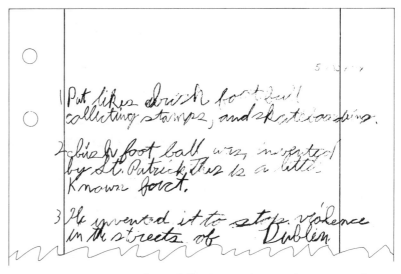

A youngster may also have difficulty working with maps, confusing north and south, east and west. He or she may confuse the size of countries and continents, for example, thinking Canada is the whole continent or the whole continent is the United States. He may not remember where countries are on an unmarked map because he cannot visualize them in his mind.

There was the case of Ginny, a bright, well-traveled girl of 14 who was failing in social studies. She did not know east from west and had no sense of direction. She thought Asia was north of New York City. Ginny was literally lost in space.

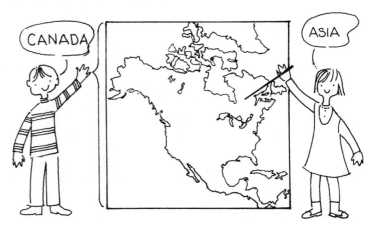

The problem of spatial relations and laterality—sense of direction, right and left—may persist all through life. In the middle grades a child may have trouble aligning his numbers in math. Mary added 2 and 5 when she should have added 3 and 5.

$$\begin{array}{r} 2\,3 \\ +\ 4\,5 \\ \hline 6\ 7 \end{array}$$

Because Marty did not space his numbers correctly in setting up this subtraction problem, he borrowed from the wrong column.

$$\begin{array}{r} 3\,4\,2 \\ -\ 1\,8 \\ \hline 1\ 6\ 2 \end{array}$$

VISUAL PERCEPTION

The ability to receive visual images accurately and to identify, organize, and comprehend what they mean.

To read, a child must be able to discriminate letters. Moreover, he must be able to select them from a background of other letters. This is called figure-ground ability—a skill we use when we read a word on a page of words or look up a word in the dictionary.

A child showing a definite lag in figure-ground and visual discrimination might not find the letters asked. He might know the alphabet but might select the wrong letters when trying to identify them. He might reverse the b *and* d *or invert the* m *and* w.

An average second-grader would be expected to read the following words:

saw

play

thing

A child with a definite lag in the area of visual perception and ordering might read:

was   (for saw)

daly   (for play)

hitting   (for thing)

Spelling involves visual perception and visual memory. The average second-grader is expected to know how to spell:

stop

said

boat

A child with varying difficulties in visual perception might spell:

spot   (for stop)

siad   (for said)

baot   (for boat)

Spelling does not depend on visual perception, memory, and ordering alone. Auditory discrimination (the ability to detect subtle differences in sounds) is a factor, too. The average second-grader is expected to know how to spell:

order

button

screen

A child weak in the area of auditory perception might write:

orter (for *order*)—confusing the *t* and *d* sound

putton (for *button*)—confusing the *p* and *b* sound

spreen (for *screen*)—confusing the *spr* blend with the *scr* blend

Spelling problems can continue into the high school years, and a boy or girl with poor auditory discrimination might spell:

exaduate (for *exaggerate*)—not hearing the third syllable

literture (for *literature*)—again not hearing the third syllable

SEQUENCING

Ability to remember the order of items—given orally or visually.

The average seven-year-old is expected to be able to say the days of the week in order, an example of auditory sequencing.

The average four-year-old should be able to follow three oral directions, another form of sequencing.

 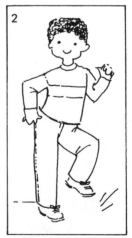 

"Erase the board." "Stamp the floor." "Bring the lunchbox."

A seven-year-old child showing a maturational lag:
- might mix up the days of the week
- might not follow directions in order
- might have difficulty remembering sentences and retelling stories.

Moreover, a seven-year-old who is definitely impaired:
- might not know the days of the week or the alphabet
- might not be able to follow any directions
- might not know in what order to put his clothes on or which comes first, lunch or supper.

Disorders of sequencing may continue into the high school years and a student:
- might still not be able to say the months in order
- might have difficulty outlining, organizing his thoughts, and writing
- might not be able to follow an author's plans.

THE CASE OF ANDY

A capsule description of Andy might be: He could talk like Winston Churchill, but he wrote like Tom Sawyer.

No one had ever suspected that Andy had learning problems as a young child. He was the shining light of a progressive California school which relegated the teaching of skills to happenstance. When he moved east and entered tenth grade, he started having trouble in English. At that point his intelligent parents, realizing he had missed out in basic skills, had him evaluated so capabilities could be assessed and areas with gaps pinpointed.

Oversized and over-intellectualized, Andy with his adult sense of humor was a delightful combination of youth and sophistication. All the kids in his class called him "The Brain." They enjoyed his jokes but feared his wit, which could be devastating. Andy was a gifted reader with a huge fund of knowledge, and his use of words was fantastic. He was a great talker—but his writing and spelling were another thing. While the contents of his compositions were creative and abstract, he had the verbosity of a Micawber, and his prose rambled on and was loaded with errors in syntax, sentence structure, and organization. His written assignments were a mess in more ways than one.

Because Andy was highly intelligent and an exceptional reader, he was able to cover up and compensate to a great extent for his specific learning disabilities. These could have resulted from premature birth; Andy was a seven-month baby.

His learning difficulties were a secret worry to the boy, and no one realized the depth of his anxiety. He knew he was bright—but felt that there must be something wrong with his brain. "Why couldn't I remember the months of the year in order? Why was learning my arithmetic tables such a frustrating task and only accomplished in seventh grade, when many dopes had mastered them in second grade?" As he grew older he had trouble learning and remembering science symbols, grammatical terms, and so on. Moreover, he was poor at following ideas in directions or making an outline. Lack of basic auditory discrimination skills affected his spelling, as did his inability to sequence the letters in a word.

Andy was greatly relieved when the nature of his difficulties was explained and he discovered that many famous men had faced similar problems in their early years. His realization that he really possessed a fine intellect despite some learning problems greatly boosted his self-confidence. As a result, he realistically accepted his problems as hurdles to be overcome by hard work. This, combined with his mature attitude and willingness to start relearning at lower levels, contributed to his progress.

Remedial lessons were planned so that the teaching of skills would be interwoven with topics that would spark interest. There would be a discussion comparing Kant's and Descartes's philosophies, followed by drill on the doubling rule in spelling. Andy never balked when it came to drills, necessary but tedious. Lessons included training in all his weak areas, with emphasis on improving written expression through phrasing topics, sentence expansion, outlining, writing succinct headlines, summarizing, and so on. Following directions was also stressed.

As was expected, Andy's attitudes and strong desire to overcome his problems were a good combination. After much hard work he made tremendous gains and learned to produce a well-organized and correctly written theme. Spelling will probably always be difficult for him, but that has improved too.

When Andy's problems were explained to his parents, with whom he had a warm, loving relationship, they felt remiss that they had been oblivious to his difficulties and had, through ignorance, disregarded obvious clues such as his not remembering his own birthday, inability to order the days of the week, poor spelling and written expression. Discovering all they could about learning disabilities, they were sympathetic, accepting, and understanding of their son's troubles without lowering their regard for his superior intellect. This positive parental attitude, combined with the continuing support of the tutor, naturally had a beneficial effect on Andy's self-image and contributed to his rapid progress.

Even though Andy had severe problems, he had a lot going for him. He was born with a high mental ability; he had no physical defect which might have retarded learning; he had a drive to succeed and was persistent in his work; he had the benefit of a stimulating cultural environment and parents who gave him attention in his early years. These are all key factors influencing learning.

There was a time when younger children who did poorly in school were thought to be stupid, lazy, or willfully inattentive. We feel many of them had learning disabilities. Nowadays we know that many children with difficulties can cope in a regular classroom if they work hard, have a good classroom teacher, have understanding parents, and obtain individual help from a warm, competent person. This would be the best situation for the learning-disabled child. Of course, children with severe disabilities need special schooling.

Older children with previously undetected learning problems can be helped, too. Those who learn that their school failures are related to specific learning problems feel much better about themselves. With help and support they learn to overcome many of their problems and compensate for others.

3 HOW DO WE HELP CHILDREN WHO ARE NOT READY FOR SCHOOL LEARNING?

Summer is over and school is starting; Christine, Kevin, Diane, and David are headed for first grade. Christine can't wait. She is wondering what her teacher looks like. Giving her mother a goodbye kiss, she dashes into the school building. Kevin is just as eager to begin first grade but walks with his older brother. He already knows how to read and plans to be the shining light of his class. Diane is squeezing her mother's hand and clinging to her skirt. She has been dreading this day all summer. David almost doesn't get to school. He is so slow dressing that his mother has to help him finish. Then on the way to school, he chases a cat, stumbles over a rock, and falls in the mud.

Mrs. Todd, the teacher who is waiting for these children, is wondering about the diversity of the incoming class. She realizes that her pupils will differ in many ways. Having taught for many years, she knows youngsters have different growth timetables and develop unevenly. She is aware of those children who have birthdays in the last quarter of the year because she knows that some of them, especially boys, may be immature and not ready for school learning; they should have waited another year before entering first grade. She also knows that a few may be late bloomers regardless of their birthdays. On the plus side, she is aware that most of these children, although they like to move about, will be able to sit still for short periods of time and to concentrate on small tasks. On the other hand, experience has shown her that there are usually some immature children who will be continually hopping up from their seats, will interrupt her when she is giving directions, will not tackle anything unless they have instant success, and will want to satisfy every whim and fancy immediately. Their immature behavior will impede their learning.

Mrs. Todd plans to work with the individual students in her class to determine how well they have developed the basic skills for school learning. She expects that many have acquired these abilities through experiences in the home environment and in kindergarten. However, every year she has some children who lag in different areas of learning—some as a result of deprivation, others because of slow development. She has also learned that deprivation is not restricted to the poor. The children from middle-class or wealthy homes who are continually left with indifferent baby-sitters may be just as disadvantaged.

What are the skills that a child must acquire in order to learn to read, to write, to spell, to do arithmetic, and to understand social studies? He must be aware of his own body and its parts and know right and left on himself (Body Image, Laterality). He needs to know directions, such as, right–left, up–down, forward–backward, east–west, north–south (Directionality). He also needs small muscle coordination for eye–hand tasks (Visual-Motor Skills). In addition, he will have to be able to identify and understand what he sees and hears (Perceptual Skills). Fundamental to all these skills is the ability to comprehend ideas and language (Conceptual Skills and Language).

BODY IMAGE, LATERALITY, DIRECTIONALITY

A child sees himself as the center of his world. It is through his own body that a child becomes oriented in space. Recognition of the two sides of the body helps to establish a sense of laterality and the concept of right and left. This is the basis of directionality, which develops with maturity.

Directionality is important for reading and writing as well as for arithmetic and social studies. A child has to distinguish between letters facing in different directions, such as *d* and *b,* and then read from left to right. In arithmetic, on the other hand, addition and subtraction problems must be computed from right to left. This is hard for a child who is not certain which direction is which. Later on, children who cannot master directionality have difficulty reading maps in social studies. By the time a child is six or seven he is expected to know right and left. He learns this first on himself, then on an object, and finally on other people.

A simple game of *Simon Says* will tell a lot about a child's knowledge of body parts and sense of laterality. Asking a child to touch his wrists, wave his right hand or hop on his left foot will soon show you if he is confused about body parts or direction.

In beginning reading and writing, and as late as second grade, we expect children to reverse letters and numbers to some extent. However, we must be alert and recognize directional problems when they continue.

Techniques for Improving Body Image and Directionality

1. Have the very young child look in a mirror and watch his arms and legs move. (This is just to notice body parts.)

2. Have the very young child lie on the floor. Outline his body with chalk. As you do this, name the parts of the body that you are outlining. Later on, see if the child can point them out.

3. Make a cardboard cut-out of the back of a boy or girl. Then cut out arms and legs and attach them to the back with paper fasteners. Draw a line down the middle of the figure. Label the two sides right (R) and left (L). Ask the child to match the positions of his body with those of the cardboard figure. (Use a paper doll as a model.)

4. Have a child roll a large ball with her right hand and then with her left hand. Later on, the child can bounce the ball with her right and left hands.

5. Draw a line down the middle of a large piece of paper or newspaper. Label the two sides right and left. Have the child drive a little car to the right and to the left.

6. Play *Simon Says*.

7. Play *Looby Lou*.

8. Have the child trace his right and left hands on a piece of paper and then label the drawings.

9. Have a child identify right and left on himself and on a doll.

10. Have a child give a doll a pretend bath, with the doll's back to the child and facing him. Ask the child to bathe certain parts of the body, stressing right and left. Have an older child act as a coach giving a team player conditioning exercises, emphasizing right and left.

11. Give directions which include "right" and "left."
    In class, draw an arrow on the board from left to right to denote direction for writing. Do this on a child's paper.
    Ask children to write their names on the left side of a paper, the date on the right.
    When the child is setting the table at home or at school, have him learn to say "Fork on the left, knife on right."

When storing food supplies in the kitchen, have the child put cereal in the right-hand cupboard, rice in the left-hand cupboard. Do this when putting supplies away at school.

12. In a group of words on a line, have the child choose the ones on that line that are the same as the one in the box:

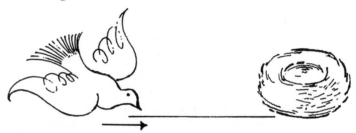

13. Have the child draw a line from a bird or animal to its home, going from left to right:

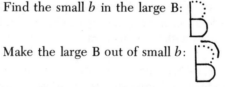

14. If a person always wears something on his left hand, like a watch or a rope bracelet, point out that this will help him remember his left hand.

15. To help establish directionality, and avoid reversals:
Find the small *b* in the large B:

Make the large B out of small *b*:

Trace the letter *b* on the child's back; have him write it down. Do this with other letters he might reverse—for example, *d*—or invert—for example, *m* and *w*, *n* and *u*.

Trace the letter *b* in the child's hand; have him write it down. Do this with other letters that he confuses.

For some, the phrase "Be right" might help the child remember that he goes to the right.

Make the letters a child is reversing or inverting out of clay or pipe cleaners; have the child trace them and then write them down. Take one letter at a time.

16. Directional confusion can affect the older student in different areas, such as handwriting, spelling, social studies, and arithmetic. See the chapters on these subjects for techniques to use.

VISUAL-MOTOR SKILLS

A child needs good small-muscle coordination in order to cut paper, to stay between the lines in coloring, to copy a design or a shape or a letter. The following chart illustrates what shapes a child is usually expected to copy at different age levels.

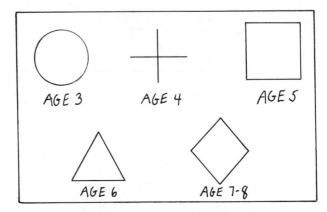

The reason readiness books stress copying shapes is that, if a child cannot copy shapes, later he will probably have difficulty copying letters. For example, if he cannot form the angles or make the diagonals on the diamond ◇ he may have trouble with such letters as Y, N, and Z. This problem is fairly common among children with severe visual-motor problems.

A lag in the visual-motor area can easily be seen by watching how a child colors and the way he copies shapes and letters. A four-to-five-year-old can draw with a pencil or crayon. A five-to-six-year-old should be able to print simple words.

A child who has poor muscle coordination may be a fine athlete, because small and gross muscle coordination are not related. Nevertheless, a learning-disabled child may have gross motor difficulties. He may not be able to skip, hop on one foot, or throw and catch a ball. While these skills are not related to reading and writing, they are very important to the child. Lags in this area of development greatly lower his self-image, and this in turn affects his school learning. Therefore, he should be helped to develop gross motor skills so he can participate adequately in gym and play games with his peers.

Techniques to Improve Visual-Motor Skills

1. Have a child practice staying within the lines in coloring books. Have a child cut out pictures or shapes that he has drawn.

2. For using small muscles, have the child:
   - sort different-sized buttons
   - make paper-clip chains
   - play pick-up sticks
   - string small wooden beads
   - make pegboard designs
   - sew sewing cards
   - put puzzles together
   - string macaroni
   - play with finger puppets

3. Draw a square, a triangle, and a diamond on the blackboard. If the child has difficulty copying them, cut the shapes out of a piece of cardboard and have him trace inside the opening:

4. Take pipe cleaners and have the child form letters with them.

5. Use Mortite, a window sealer, to form letters. Then have the child feel them; later write them.

6. Use soft clay for the same purpose.

7. Take a shoebox. Put sand or sugar in it. Have the child trace shapes and letters in it.

8. For additional visual-motor skills involving handwriting, see Chapter 9.

9. Ask the child to draw a line on a path, going from one end to the other. Explain that "on the path" means within the dark lines. Make your own paths. These are examples:

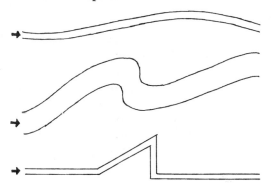

PERCEPTUAL SKILLS

Perceptual skills are the main tools for early learning. Jimmy cannot remember what the letters look like and reads *d* for *b* and *w* for *m*. Patty has trouble discriminating sounds. To her the word *van* sounds like *fan*. Both Johnny and Patty have perceptual problems, Johnny in the visual area, Patty in the auditory area. Both of them may have difficulty learning to read and write, and they may have to be taught by different methods. When we talk about visual and auditory perception, we mean an individual's ability to identify and interpret what he sees and hears. Generally speaking, the greatest perceptual growth takes place between the ages of three and seven. The sequence of development is from the general to the specific. We are not referring to visual or hearing acuity. Of course, visual or hearing impairment can interfere greatly with learning. Vision and hearing should be checked at an early age.

Since we learn through sight and sound, any visual or auditory defects can impair all types of discrimination and impede learning. Nowadays babies' eyes can be tested during infancy and treated successfully, even for such conditions as cataracts and amblyopia (lazy eye). Muscle weakness may prevent a child's two eyes from working together harmoniously, resulting in visual distortions. This, in turn, may limit his visual discrimination and may make it difficult for him to hold the line in reading. No matter how slight, muscle weakness should never be ignored. Depending on its severity, it can be corrected by eyeglasses, a series of orthoptic exercises, or an operation. Unfortunately, eye muscle weakness is not uncommon in learning-disabled children.

Generally, hearing is tested when a child enters school. If further testing is needed, the child will be referred to a clinic or an audiologist. Parents should be aware that if constant colds and secondary bacterial infections have caused a child to be hard of hearing, there is medical treatment which can relieve the blockage and enable a child to improve his hearing. Results, in many cases, have been excellent. For Bobby, it changed his life—from being a reticent, nonachieving child he became a happy boy who suddenly made great strides in reading.

Visual Perception

A child sees with his eyes but understands with his brain. The infant first explores his world just through his senses—moving, touching, hearing, seeing. Later on, he is able to identify an object visually and make an association with it. For example, a baby crawling in the kitchen touches the stove and feels that it is too hot. If the next time he is in the kitchen, he just looks at the stove and does not touch it, in all likelihood he has remembered an unpleasant association. This is the primitive beginning of what we call visual perception. Perception commences only when the baby can look at an object, recognize it and remember his association with it. There has to be at least one association stored in his memory bank; otherwise, it is not perception. As the baby grows, he will learn to recognize familiar objects in his room from associations: his cup, his teddy bear, his crib. The next step will be his ability to identify pictures of these objects in a book. During the preschool years he will become familiar with different shapes—a circle, a square, a triangle—and will learn to recognize similarities and differences between them. Finally he will be able to recognize letters and identify and discriminate words.

DEVELOPMENT OF VISUAL DISCRIMINATION

At the age of three and sometimes earlier, a child is expected to discriminate between objects and find two that look alike.

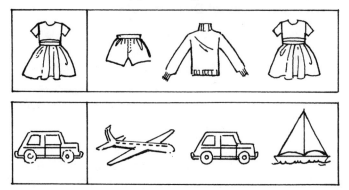

At the age of four, a child is expected to distinguish the difference between shapes. He has to be able to do this before he can make a distinction between letters. For example, it is easier for him to discriminate between the square and the triangle than to recognize the H and A.

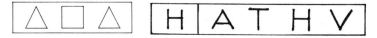

Around the age of five a child is expected to match letters.

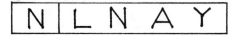

By the time a child is six, he is expected to differentiate between letters that can be rotated.

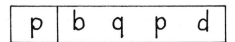

Also, by six, a child is usually able to recognize two- and three-letter words that are similar.

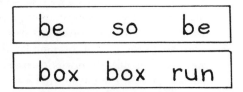

We can gauge a child's development in visual discrimination by observing his or her performance on these tasks.

Techniques to Improve
Visual Discrimination

1. Sort the following:
   Boxes according to size
   Buttons and blocks according to size and color
   Toy beads according to shape and color
   Plastic knives, forks, spoons according to kind
   Cans according to size
   Shells according to type

   The following six activities are similar to ones found in readiness programs. You can use them as models if you wish to make your own materials.

2. Ask the child to match the forms that are alike:

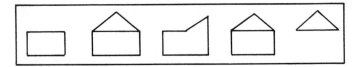

3. Ask the child to match designs that are alike:

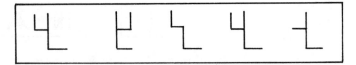

4. Ask the child to circle letters that are alike:

$$n \quad m \quad m \quad h \quad u \quad m$$

5. Ask the child to connect letters that are alike:

6. Ask the child to match words that are alike:

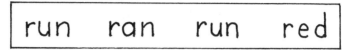

7. Ask the child to choose which word is different:

8. Using wooden or plastic letters, have the child sort them, picking out the *f*'s, the *t*'s; touching and tracing them with his fingers will help him to recognize them.

For the older person

9. Have him do jigsaw puzzles of varying difficulty, starting with simpler puzzles.

10. Have him find syllables that are alike in a group of words:
    *pen*cil
    inde*pen*dent
    hap*pen*

11. Select prefixes that are alike in a group of words. (Use a dictionary for choosing the words.)
    *un*tie   inland
    repay   *un*able
    *un*fold   export

12. Select suffixes that are alike in a group of words. (Again, use the dictionary for the words.)
    law*ful*   pleasant
    likable   musical
    skill*ful*   trust*ful*

13. Play the *Third Syllable* game (produced by Educational Aids, 845 Wisteria Drive, Freemont, CA 94538). The purpose of this game is to match the words which have the same third syllable. For example: enerv*va*ting, elev*va*ting.

Visual Figure-Ground

Another aspect of visual perception is the ability to distinguish an object from its background. We call this figure–ground. This skill involves focusing attention on the required items without being distracted by irrelevant background details.

If a child is going to derive any meaning from a picture, he has to learn to focus on the main object in the picture. When a child is asked to give the following picture a name, and he says, "chocolate ice cream cone," we know he has not grasped the main idea. He should have focused on the man selling ice cream to the children.

Most likely, this same child would have had difficulty finding the two hidden kittens in this picture:

It is more difficult for a child with figure–ground problems to find the different objects when they are jumbled in a picture:

Attending to the object becomes even more important when a child has to focus on one word at a time set in a whole page of words, and even more difficult when he has to focus on small parts of words. Many children and adults are confused and bothered by too much on a page. Some of the mimeographed sheets used in schools and offices hinder instead of help.

Dictionary and encyclopedia work present problems for any student or adult with figure–ground problems. All through life figure–ground discrimination is a valuable tool: when we skim for a number in the telephone book, read a timetable to discover if the 5:38 train is still running, or search for an item in the supermarket, we have to distinguish an object from its background.

Techniques to Improve Visual Figure–Ground Ability

1. Ask the child to find as many rectangles in a room as he can. Examples: tabletop, picture, rug, window pane.

2. Ask the child to find as many circular objects as he can in a room. Examples: clock, coaster, base of lamp.

3. Look in a store window and ask the child to pick out particular items.

4. Have the child find items you need in the supermarket.

5. Take an advertisement from a newspaper and ask the child to find particular items:

6. Ask the child to find hidden pictures in puzzle books and children's magazines.

For the older student

7. Start training the student in the use of the table of contents. For example, in an American History textbook, ask him to find the chapter on the Industrial Revolution or the chapter that discusses the Spanish-American War. Have him practice using chapter headings and subheadings.

8. Have the student practice skimming for certain facts. Use short selections.

9. Take a newspaper and ask a student to find headlines on special subjects—for example, a financial crisis, a murder, a sports event.

10. Take the television listings and ask the student to search for different programs, or for the availability of programs at certain hours.

11. Have the student practice reading timetables; start with local train schedules and work up to international airline schedules.

Visual Memory

Visual memory is a very important aspect of visual perception. A child has to remember first, what objects and shapes look like, then letters, and finally words. At a higher level, a student must remember sentences and paragraphs when he studies; otherwise, he will have to reread constantly.

Memory is an active process that requires attention and reinforcement. Many people with weak visual memories have to be helped to develop their visual imagery. Some cannot make any mental pictures.

A four-year-old is expected to remember one of three familiar objects removed from view, and answer the question "Which one did I hide?"

A five-to-six-year-old is expected to be able to identify missing parts of familiar objects:

An eight-to-nine-year-old is expected to copy a phrase similar to the following from memory, after looking at it for 15 seconds: big airplanes and loud jets.

A ten-to-eleven-year-old is expected to copy designs similar to the following from memory:

Techniques to Improve Visual Memory

1. Many children with a poor memory for letters and words are surprised when they can remember their favorite TV show and describe what the characters look like. Have the child pretend he has a TV camera in his head and that things flash in his mind and he can remember them. A mental picture combined with a meaningful association will also help his visual memory: *T with a friend called Tommy*

2. Show the child a picture from a book or magazine; remove it and ask the child to describe it—immediately, and after a period of time.

3. Take two objects and place them in a certain position. Have the child look at them; remove them and then have the child put them back in the same place. (You can do this with three, four, and five objects.)

4. Play a party game. Put a number of objects on a tray. Have the child look at them. Remove the tray of objects. Ask the child to name as many of them as he can recall.

5. Have the child look at you for a few seconds. Then ask her to close her eyes. Ask her if she can remember what you are wearing.

6. Find the missing parts in pictures:

For the older student

7. Adapt the above activities to the older student.

8. Practice improving memory with pictures. In the following picture of a purse-snatching, ask the student to be a witness to the incident. Show him the picture for a few minutes; then have him describe what happened. He must be specific if he is to be a good witness.

9. Suggest to the student that she use colored markers to underline or number important parts of her notes.

10. Have the child practice remembering license plates. He can pretend

he is a policeman. Suggest that grouping the letters and numbers aids memory: *HBH — 223*

Auditory Perception

Many components of visual perception are inherent in auditory perception. Assuming that a child's hearing acuity is normal, how and what does he hear? What does he understand when he is listening? The development of auditory perception is so intertwined with language that it will be discussed in depth in the chapter on language. Before a child is able to learn to read phonetically, he must progress through certain steps in his auditory development. First of all, he must be able to distinguish sounds in the environment—a door banging, a bird chirping, a bell ringing. Next, he must be able to rhyme; then he must be able to discriminate between different letter sounds—for example, *f* and *v*—and finally he must be able to recognize the distinctions between different words—for example, *sat* and *bat, order* and *auto*.

DEVELOPMENT OF AUDITORY PERCEPTION

At an early age a child is expected to be able to rhyme. In these two pictures, a child is expected to be able to select the two objects that rhyme: in (1) mop and top, in (2) tree and bee.

Between five and six a child is expected to be able to hear the differences between the sounds of letters. For example, he is expected to be able to select objects that begin with the same sound: in (3) sock, saw, sun; in (4) ball, box, boat.

Once he has learned a letter and its sound, he is expected to be able to match the letter to the picture beginning with that letter sound: T and turtle. Associating a sound with its letter is a real hurdle for many children, especially those with an auditory weakness.

This step is a little harder. The child has to write the letter that starts the name of the picture. He has to recall the sound he hears at the beginning of the word, know what letter goes with the sound, and reproduce it in writing. This combination of skills is necessary for reading and spelling.

We can gauge a child's development in auditory discrimination by observing his performance on the tasks just described.

In addition, a child's speech may be an important indicator of problems in this area. Listen to how he talks. Does he say *dop* for *top* or call his *puppy* a *bubby*? Be alert and determine whether he has an auditory or speech problem. Perhaps he has both. An older student's compositions and spelling will clue you in as to how he hears sounds. Does he write *emeny* for *enemy*, or *flustrate* for *frustrate*?

Techniques to Improve Auditory Discrimination

1. Have the child close his eyes and identify sounds you make. Examples: blow whistle, ring bell, bang drum.

2. Have the child close his eyes. Drop objects on the floor or table. Have the child guess what they are. Examples: pencil, book, can, coin.

3. Have the child imitate rhythm patterns that you make: Tap with a pencil or clap with your hands. Examples:

   – – – – – – – – / – – – – – – – –

4. Have the child finish a familiar nursery rhyme. Be sure to tell him that rhymes are words that end with the same sound.

   Jack be nimble, Jack be quick
   Jack jump over the _____. *(candle*stick)

5. Have the child complete a two-line rhyme:

   Let us look
   At a _____. *(book)*

6. In a group of pictures, have the child pick out the two that rhyme:

7. Ask the child to answer riddles that involve rhyming words:

   It rhymes with *horn,* but you can eat it. (corn)
   Tell me a flower that rhymes with *nose.* (rose)

8. Draw a ladder. On each rung write a word. Have the child shake two dice; move a button to the rung of the ladder whose number corresponds with the number on the dice. Ask the child to think of a word that rhymes with the word on that rung. Repeat this. Score the number of words she produces correctly.

12	ten
11	hit
10	ran
9	top
8	cut
7	had
6	let
5	win
4	fun
3	not
2	sip
1	mat

9. Say a word. Ask the child to repeat the sound he hears.

at the beginning,	foot (*sound* of *f*)
in the middle,	fat (*sound* of short *a*)
at the end,	jump (*sound* of *p*)

10. Take a box of small toys and ask the child to repeat the sounds he hears in their names—at the beginning, in the middle, at the end of their names.

11. In a group of pictures, ask the child to select the ones that begin with the same sound.

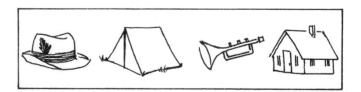

12. Say a pair of words to a child. Ask him if they are alike, or different.

cap—map	set—set
his—his	sit—sat

13. The step in auditory discrimination which involves associating a *letter* with its *sound* is taken up in Chapter 5, in the section on teaching letter sounds.

14. The above techniques can be adapted to the older student with an auditory discrimination problem.

Auditory Figure-Ground

Just as many children cannot visually discriminate an object from its background, there are some children who cannot select auditorily the important words and main ideas when listening to people talk. These are the children who most of the time do not have the foggiest idea what a teacher is talking about and have difficulty following directions. In addition, many of them have trouble listening to a person when there is background noise. They are unable to screen out superfluous sounds. A good teacher will make herself understood through extensive discussion with these children until they grasp her ideas and directions.

Techniques to Improve Auditory Figure–Ground

1. Play a game with a child in which you ask him to *listen* to a list of words and to pick out certain ones that you specify.

    EXAMPLES
    In the following list, can you pick out the animals that generally do not live in a house?

lion	dog
mouse	elephant
cat	rabbit
kangaroo	bear

    In the following list, can you pick out the vegetables?

oranges	grapes
peas	cherries
string beans	carrots
apples	lettuce

2. Read a short story to the child. At the end, ask him to choose the best title out of a group you suggest to him.

    EXAMPLE

    John, Tom, and Billy are ice skating on the safe side of the lake. Soon they see a little boy on the other side of the lake, near the danger sign.

He falls through the ice. Tom and John start yelling for help. Billy goes to the boy's rescue and saves him. Billy lies down on the ice and is able to reach him with a board.

Which is the best title:

1. Three Boys Go Ice Skating
2. Billy Saves a Little Boy*
3. A Little Boy Falls In

3. Tell the child or older student that you are going to say four sentences, but only one makes sense. Ask him to tell you which one makes sense.

FOR THE YOUNGER CHILD

Tommy has 20 toes.
The cat barks.
The children like to play games.*
She put a baseball in the dishwasher.

FOR THE OLDER STUDENT

Ann plans to study the French Revolution in science class.
They watched the news program on the radio.
The boys are betting on the Yankees to win.*
John saved his money to sell his second-hand car.

Auditory Memory

Basically, auditory memory falls into two categories, short- and long-term. In general, children and adults have adequate short-term memories. However, many with learning problems may have difficulty with all types of memory, especially recalling names, symbols, verbal and numerical facts, definitions, and meaning and usage of language over a period of time. This can be a handicap because much of academic learning and adult business depends on long-term memory—arithmetic facts, dates for history, names for parts of speech, scientific symbols, formulas, and so on. From babyhood on, a human being is developing his memory.

AUDITORY VERBAL MEMORY

A three-to-four-year-old is expected to remember nursery rhymes.

A five-year-old is expected to repeat a sentence of twelve syllables, such as "Jack wants a big red fire engine for his birthday."

An eight-year-old is expected to repeat a sentence of sixteen syllables, such as "Beth went to the new theater in town to see The Sound of Music."

AUDITORY NUMERICAL MEMORY

A four-to-five-year-old is expected to repeat four digits forward.
A seven-to-eight-year-old is expected to repeat five digits forward.
An eight-to-ten-year-old is expected to repeat four digits reversed.
A ten-to-fifteen-year-old is expected to repeat five digits reversed.

Activities to Improve Auditory Memory

1. Have the child close her eyes. Bounce a ball; see if she can tell how many times you bounced it.

2. Read a short story to the child. Ask him salient questions.

3. Have the child pretend she is a shopkeeper. You be the customer. Order some items from her. See if she can remember them.

4. Have a youngster pretend to be a waiter or waitress—who doesn't write down an order. See how much he can recall of an order you give him. (Some children need to clue themselves in by thinking of the number of things that were ordered, or by thinking of the first letter of the items.)

5. For an older child: Suggest that she listen for cue words that will help her recall important ideas:

   then, next, finally
   as a result, consequently
   also, in addition
   first, second, third

6. Auditory memory aids visual memory and vice versa.[1]

   EXAMPLE
   Show a child several related pictures, such as pictures of different birds. Say the names for him and ask him to repeat them while looking at them. Remove the pictures and ask him to recall the names.

Visual and Auditory Sequencing

We sequence or order every day of our lives. At home, we sequence when we follow a recipe, follow a dress pattern, repair a bicycle, or assemble a stereo set. At the office, we file all kinds of papers alphabetically; we follow daily routines and procedures that are well ordered. The school child is

---

[1]The subject of memory, particularly for the older student, will be discussed in depth in Chapter 10.

constantly involved in tasks that demand order. He must learn his ABC's, learn to count, learn the days of the week and the months of the year, learn to tell time; and he must follow directions. As he gets older, he must outline his reading material, outline his compositions; he must do his scientific experiments in sequential order according to correct procedures. Above all, he must organize his work. This is difficult for many people, especially the learning-disabled, who can be immature and disorganized.

Visual and auditory sequencing are closely related and both involve *memory* and *attention.* For example, a young child in first grade usually *sees* large letters of the alphabet posted above the blackboard. He also *hears* his teacher say the letters in order. Perhaps he hears her singing the alphabet song. When a child learns to order the days of the week or the months of the year, he uses visual and auditory means to help him remember them.

Many bright youngsters, even though they have excellent language comprehension, cannot follow commands because of their limited memory and inability to recall a series. These students, young and old, may have trouble remembering a teacher's instructions or assignments. As adults, they will not be competent on the job if they do not learn to follow directions.

VISUAL SEQUENCING

A six-year-old is expected to copy a chain of beads from memory.

Around six a child is expected to be able to put a series of pictures in the proper order to tell a story. (The pictures in the illustration are not in order.)

An eight-to-ten-year-old is expected to put a series of pictures in the proper order to tell a more complicated story. (The pictures in the illustration are not in order.)

At or by the age of six a child is expected to write the numbers 1–11 (or more) in order.

At or by the age of seven a child is expected to write the numbers 1–20 in order.

A six-to-seven-year-old is expected to write the numbers 0–50 in order.

AUDITORY SEQUENCING

A four-to-five-year-old is expected to follow three directions in order.

A six-to-eight-year-old is expected to follow four directions in order.

A five-year-old is expected to tell a story accurately.

A six-to-eight-year-old is expected to name the days of the week in order.

A seven-to-eight-year-old is expected to name the months of the year in order.

A four-year-old is expected to count to 5.

At or by six a child is expected to count to 30.

At six to seven a child is expected to count to 100.

Techniques to Improve Visual Sequencing

1. Have the child do symbol discrimination and sequencing. In this exercise, he must cross out the two items he sees at the top of the page. To do this, he must go from left to right and mark the star and the circle in the sequence in which he sees them.

2. String a series of beads using different colors and/or shapes. Have the child string a set of beads in the same order as yours.

3. In a chain of beads that has been drawn on paper, have a youngster continue drawing the chain, keeping the same pattern.

4. Write the alphabet. Write numbers in order.

5. Use follow-the-dot books.

6. Cut up a comic strip into individual pictures. Present them in the wrong order. Have the child sequence them so they make sense.

7. Have the youngster do letter tracking (see page 44). In this exercise, he must cross out the alphabet in proper sequence, going from left to right.

stil onap cred myf(b)x m(c)hez togu
j(d)(e)k pyx wrog ilz v(f)smolt nik
truz(g)mp(h)b tawp vox sanc quork
fyrz tuc (i)e b(j)paz wre(k)tux dof
wabs h(l)t(m)g(n)d tev b(o)er fatz
g(p)y bast(qu)ack gax sich(r)baf biz
jalf deb(s)(t)h gok chay (k)(u)en mib
nep bafil(v)b chone ply d(w)c grik
cro(x)ah strel(y)be m(z)quelp noch

8. Have the child select the correct order of letters in words.

rac   arc   car

Activities to Improve
Auditory Sequencing

1. Have the child practice reciting the alphabet. Have him sing it—
rhythm always helps.

2. Have the child count numbers.

3. Beat a rhythmic pattern on a drum. Have the child reproduce it on the
drum.

— — — — — — / — — — — — — —

(If he needs help, have him look at the visual pattern, like the one
above.)

4. With an older child, use the Morse Code. Tell him what it means.

• • • / – – – / • • • = SOS
(S)   (O)   (S)

5. Have the child practice remembering telephone numbers. Use those of
family and friends to make it more meaningful. Show him how grouping
helps his memory.

326–1313

6. Have the child repeat sentences after you. Begin with short sentences;

increase them in length. Build on the same subject as shown below.

The boys play.

The boys play Frisbee.

The boys play Frisbee in the street.

The eighth-grade boys play Frisbee in the street after school.

7. Following instructions: For the young child, begin with paper and pencil tasks.

Example: Present him with a series of animal pictures and ask him to draw a line around a dog and put an X above the pony.

Next, give directions that involve movement. For example, tell him, "Stamp your foot. Clap your hands." Gradually increase the number of directions to three or four and always remember to speak slowly and clearly.

8. In school, a child is constantly bombarded with directions—going to assemblies, participating in fire drills, changing classes, doing daily assignments. Some children do not seem to be able to do what they are told. A teacher's aide or volunteer can be helpful. He or she can practice following a series of instructions with the child, in various school situations.

9. If an older student cannot grasp oral assignments fast enough to write them in his notebook, he needs help. Either someone in school can write the assignment for him, or a parent can get the weekly assignments from the teacher. (This is a necessary crutch. Hopefully, it will be only temporary.)

It must be apparent that none of the basic skills is taught in isolation. For example, when the children are doing work in a readiness book that might depend on visual activities, like matching shapes, they will have to listen to oral directions as well. If a teacher tells a story, she may use a series of pictures to help her pupils remember what they hear. At a higher level, a person who is a visual learner should use his visual skills to remember what a word looks like. If he is an auditory learner, he should verbalize vocally what he wants to spell so he may recall it. In this way a person is learning through his strengths. Nevertheless, in teaching, it is necessary to identify and remediate weaknesses while building on strengths.

If a person is weak in both visual and auditory areas, he may need to reinforce skills through other methods—touching and doing. Multisensory techniques can be applied to many areas of learning. Of course, the selection of techniques will be determined by an individual's needs in special areas.

Generally, first-grade teachers concentrate first on perceptual skills because they are the main tools for the mechanics of reading and writing. In addition, teachers explore how well children understand what they see and hear, and later read. They want to discover how well the boys and girls comprehend ideas (concepts) relating to the world around them. Often, however, teachers expect that students will differ as widely in their thinking abilities as they do in their perceptual and motor skills, and understand that concepts, or thinking, depend largely on intelligence and background. For instance, a child who has just moved from a midwestern farm will understand the significance of seasons—spring for planting crops, summer for growing them, fall for harvesting them, winter for planning. On the other hand, the seasons will mean little to a child who, since birth, has lived in a southern city, where the grass is always green, flowers always bloom, and snow rarely falls.

Teachers realize that conceptual development is a real struggle for learning-disabled children because they are so literal. Take Sam, who, when his teacher said "Spring is coming," waved his hand and cried out, "I didn't know spring had feet."

A child requires well-developed language skills before he is ready for school learning. This means he has to understand what other people are saying, and must be able to express his thoughts in simple but well-organized sentences. Because the development of language is basic to the development of concepts, the two cannot be separated; so we will discuss them as a unit in the next chapter. As Samuel Johnson said, "Language is the dress of thought."

MATERIALS SUGGESTED

1. *ABC Mazes*, Waneta B. Bullock and Ganelle Loveless, Ann Arbor Publishers, Inc., Naples, Fla. 33940.

2. *Advantage*, Raymond Fournier and Vincent Presno, Prentice-Hall, Inc., Englewood Cliffs, N.J. 07632.

3. *All About Me Books* (Boy, Girl), Frank E. Richards Publishing Co., Inc., Phoenix, N.Y. 13135.

4. *Ann Arbor Tracking Program*, Ann Arbor Publishers, Inc., Naples, Fla. 33940. Symbol Discrimination and Sequencing; Letter Tracking.

5. *Developmental Program in Visual Perception*, Marianne Frostig, Follett Publishing Co., Chicago, Ill.

6. *Excel*, Experience for Children in Learning I, II, Polly Behrman, Joan Millman, Educators Publishing Service, Inc., Cambridge, Mass. 02138.

7. *Kindergarten Fun*, Mary Ambrose, Prentice-Hall, Inc., Englewood Cliffs, N.J. 07632.

8. *The Maze Book*, Paul McCreary, Ann Arbor Publishers, Inc., Naples, Fla. 33940.

9. *A Multisensory Approach to Language Arts,* Beth Slingerland, Educators Publishing Service, Cambridge, Mass. 02138.

10. *Perceptual Activities,* Paul McCreary, Ann Arbor Publishers, Inc., Naples, Fla. 33940.

11. *Sequential Cards—By Color, Shape and Size,* Incentive for Learning, Inc., 800 West Van Buren St., Chicago, Ill. 60607.

12. *Sequential Cards—Levels I, II, III,* Incentive for Learning, Inc., Chicago, Ill. 60607.

13. *Weekly Reader Books and Teaching Aids,* Xerox Education Publications, Columbus, Ohio 43216. *Zip's Book of Animals; Zip's Book of Wheels; Zip's Book of Puzzles; First Step to Reading; Buddy's Book of Puzzles.*

4 THINKING AND LANGUAGE

THINKING

Young children think differently from adults. Because of their immaturity and lack of experience they are often confused. Generally their lack of understanding is not spotted until they do or say something comical:

> *Sally watered her kitten every day to make it grow.*
>
> *After David sang "My Country 'Tis of Thee" at school, he asked, "How far is 'Tis of Thee from Chicago?"*

Concepts (the understanding of objects, situations, words, and ideas) change at different maturity levels. Consider, for example, a ride in an automobile. To the baby, it means a fun outing; she gets excited when she sees her mother take out her car keys. Later on, a ride means going shopping with her mother. Still later, it means a lift to school or to parties; riding saves the youngster from walking. At long last, she learns to drive, one of the most exciting moments in her life. She is on her own and senses her power. But what does a car represent to the mother who is constantly driving? It is not so enchanting. She feels like a taxi driver.

Understanding different maturity levels in thinking is important for everyone dealing with children. Most of the time adults, parents and teachers, assume that children's thinking is more mature than it really is. As a result, sometimes teachers do not realize that children need more explanation, and sometimes parents do not realize that they need less. In answering questions, parents generally go far beyond the answers children require. When twelve-year-old Shirley asked what rape meant, her mother went into a biological dissertation. When she finished, she asked, "But why do you want to know?" Shirley replied, "I don't understand the social studies book when it says that the lumberman raped the forest."

Concepts also depend on experiences and background. Two twelve-year-old girls were being tested by the school psychologist. To the question why we should give to organized charity, one youngster quickly replied, "Because it's a tax deduction." Her family seemed to equate charity with tax deductions. The other girl said, "Charity is wonderful because it helps people when they are in trouble." Her family had gone through hard times and had been helped financially.

Through the years, researchers have been probing the complexities of the brain. Many clues have surfaced, but how the brain actually works remains a mystery. We have, however, become fairly knowledgeable about the growth of intelligence and understanding, which develop in sequential stages like every phase of maturation. How does this growth begin? How does a little newborn infant completely dependent on others become a thinking, comprehending human being?

Piaget, the French psychologist, claims that when a baby crawls about and explores the world by touching, tasting, and looking (sensory motor activities), he or she is developing the foundation for all future thinking.

Let's take the baby and the stove again. In the previous chapter we discussed the baby who avoided touching the stove in the kitchen. The only association he had with a stove was heat. But later, as he grew older and played around the kitchen, he noticed other things about the stove—his mother could make a flame on the stove; she could use the stove to cook his food. As time went on, he realized that a stove, sink, and refrigerator belong together. Relating his observations and remembering them resulted in his gradually acquiring a fairly good concept of a stove.

Children's experiences, of course, are limited. In the process of developing concepts, they make haphazard associations and false analogies. When two-year-old Brooke saw her cousin blow on the reed of her clarinet, she squealed, "Hot, hot." Little Brooke's only experience with blowing was cooling off hot cocoa. "I know the difference between Mommies and Daddies," piped up four-year-old David as he watched his father emerge from the shower. "Tell me," replied his father. "Mommies wear lipstick," said David seriously.

Preschool children judge the world by appearances and sometimes seem rather foolish. Moreover, they do not realize that other people see things from a viewpoint different from their own; preschoolers see the world only in relation to themselves. Two-year-old Mike climbed out of his crib one night and stealthily crept out of his room; when he heard his grandmother coming his way, he backed against the wall and covered his eyes with his hands. Mike thought that because he could not see her, she could not see him. When five-year-old Art took his first ride in an airplane and looked down, he cried, "See all the toy houses and cars on the ground." Art did not understand that houses and cars look small only from a distance, because he did not stop to think about how far away he was from the ground.

Polly and Jack, five-year-olds, were given two identical packages of M & M's. Polly spilled hers all over the table; Jack left his in a neat pile. Polly crowed, "I have more than you have." "I've been gypped," Jack shrieked. Jack and Polly could not understand that the amount stays the same even though appearances change.

According to Piaget, at six or seven most children put on their thinking caps and start analyzing what they see. They are becoming social beings and no longer believe that the world revolves around them. A seven-year-old would not feel she had more M & M's because they were scattered over the table. From seven to eleven, children become able to relate parts to the whole and therefore are able to learn arithmetic, reading, writing, and spelling. They are able to reason about these subjects on a concrete level. As they progress in school, they are expected to acquire more difficult concepts, such as categorizing, selecting the main idea of a picture or a story, identifying cause and effect, drawing conclusions, making comparisons and predicting the outcome of events of a story. As adolescents, they should be ready to cope with abstract reasoning. They will learn to reflect on possibilities and make thoughtful choices. This all leads to pragmatic and abstract thinking at an adult level.[1]

The transition period from the preschool unanalytical stage to real thinking is a gradual process. Children have different timetables in crossing this bridge, but generally master the process without too many hurdles. In contrast, many learning-disabled children struggle through this crucial

[1]For further reading on Jean Piaget's contribution to children's thinking, see Millie Almy with Edward Chittenden and Paula Miller, *Young Children's Thinking* (New York: Teachers College Press, Columbia University, 1966).

period. However, they will learn to analyze in time, with meaningful experiences and good teaching.

Another difference between the learning-disabled child and the average child is in the ability to assimilate information. The average child is constantly acquiring information just by keeping his eyes and ears open; he is the proverbial "little pitcher with big ears." The learning-disabled child may not tune into this "at random education" because he is distracted by inconsequential happenings no matter where he is. For example, it is dinner time at the Spencers' house, and Mr. and Mrs. Spencer are discussing a current political election. Their ten-year-old son, Tom, listening attentively, asks thoughtful questions. Dick, who is two years older and learning-disabled, listens for a moment, but then starts playing with his black cocker spaniel, who is sitting beside him; a few minutes later he hops up from the table to pick up a scrap of paper under the door sill.

Not all families are like the Spencers. It is important to remember that children coming from a deprived environment where there is little information or mental stimulation will have less information to absorb.

There are many concepts a child should have grasped by the time he enters first grade. Among these are size, space, and time.

Size and Space

Children as well as adults grasp concepts of size more easily through concrete comparisons. In the beginning, a child is aware of size only in relation to himself. He is bigger than his puppy; his older brother is bigger than he is. As a child grows older and becomes less self-centered, he learns to understand the concept of size by observing different-sized objects around him. At home, he sees that the sofa is bigger than a chair. On the street, he sees that an automobile is larger than a motorcycle. At school, he observes that some of his classmates are larger than others.

While it is not difficult for the child to perceive the relative sizes of animals, cars, houses, etc., he finds abstract ideas of size more confusing. Schoolchildren can see the relative sizes of places on a globe but they cannot grasp the size of oceans or land forms.

A child's body is his point of reference in space as well as size. His concept of space depends on his body image and his sense of directionality. He must know left and right on himself before he can understand what is meant by "front" and "back." Children in kindergarten and first grade are expected to know what is meant by "up," "down," "forward," "backward," "under," and "above." Nevertheless, some children, especially those with learning problems, are bewildered by the meaning of these abstract words and are frequently disoriented in space. For instance, when Jimmy was asked to go to the "front" of the room for "Show and Tell," he went to the "back" of the room. When Tony was asked to put his lunch box "in" the desk, he put it "under" the desk. These two children were known to have trouble finding their way to school. When they learn to drive, there is a good possibility they will have trouble finding the right road.

For the beginning reader, the many rotated and inverted versions of similar letters naturally create problems. When a *b* turns itself around, it becomes *d*. When an *m* stands on its head, it becomes a *w*. Learning that there is one acceptable position for each letter in the English alphabet and for each number is difficult for most children. These fixed letter and number positions are particularly confusing to children with spatial problems and directional difficulties, which we discussed earlier.

Without understanding position in space the young child cannot align or group numbers correctly in arithmetic. Later on, he may have difficulty working with perimeters and areas, or setting up equations. In writing, his letters may dance above or below the lines and his words may jam together. He may never pay attention to margins. (See Chapter 9.)

This same child may have problems with geographical concepts. Map directions confound him and the association between a two-dimensional map and a three-dimensional world puzzles him. Also, he may be baffled by distances between countries, sections of continents and states, and may have trouble locating countries on a map. Although he can be taught to find places on a map, he may have difficulty forming mental images of these places.

Sam, a junior high school student in Miami, was asked to name one country bordering the United States. The answer came back, "China." When Sam was shown an unmarked map of North America, he was able to identify the countries that touched the United States and said, "Isn't it strange? I learned to find places on a map, but I can't find them in my head." Sam's problem was forming visual images. Barbara had another problem with geography. She could not grasp the relationship of a city to a state, of a state to a country, of a country to a continent. What is more, Barbara could not understand how she could be in Boston *and* in Massachusetts *and* in the United States at the same time.

While children can see which is larger, a jet plane or a helicopter, they cannot "see" which is bigger, a city or a state. To the very young child, his own home is the whole world. His concept of the world gradually comes to include the neighborhood, the school, the community in which he lives and eventually, the whole world. Adults must realize that the process by which a child comes to understand the vastness of the world takes many years.

SIZE AND SPACE DEVELOPMENTAL TIMETABLE

A four-to-five-year-old is expected:

- to recognize differences in size of objects presented to him, provided the size difference is big, for example, a large panda and a small teddy bear.
- to know the concept of space, *up, down,* etc.
- to place a series of nesting boxes in order.

A six-to-seven-year-old is expected:
- to know his neighborhood and the names of nearby streets.
- to become gradually familiar with his community.
- to show interest in places beyond his community.

An eight-to-nine-year-old is expected:
- to be able to go to familiar places on his own.
- to have a better understanding of the spatial relationships of foreign countries to one another.
- to show interest in faraway countries and in maps.

Activities to Improve Concepts of Size and Space

For the preschool child

1. Have the child put nesting blocks together according to size.

2. Have the child compare the relative sizes of household objects, such as pots and pans, measuring spoons, cans, books, shoes, gloves.

3. Have the child compare different lengths of string.

4. Have the child compare the sizes of pets, or of animals at the zoo.

For the child at school

1. Draw a castle on the board. Give the child verbal directions:

   "Draw a lake in front of the castle."
   "Draw a tree by the side of the castle."
   "Draw a flag on top of its roof."
   "Draw a soldier in front of the gate."
   "Draw a horse beside him."

2. Ask the child to illustrate different prepositions or prepositional phrases on paper: up, down, behind, in front of, on top of, in back of, and so on.

3. Ask the child to play charades, acting out prepositions.

4. In a group of similar objects, have the child match two pictures that are in the same position:

5. The type of exercise described here can be found in many readiness books. You can make your own, using objects, shapes, or letters. Be sure two figures in the group are in exactly the same position.

6. Scatter magazines on the floor. Direct the child to walk to the one nearest to him, the one nearest to you, the one farthest from him, the one farthest from you, the one behind the chair.

7. Ask the child to draw a plan of any room with furniture: classroom, bedroom, family room, living room.

8. Give the child a simple floor plan with furniture. Have him devise a treasure hunt, making up accurate clues.

9. Present the child with geographical terms:

   city
   village
   continent
   country
   state

   Ask him to write them in the correct size order, or number them in the correct order.

10. Cut out different sized circles of paper to represent a village or town, a city, a state, a country, and a continent, and fasten them together to show the relative size differences:

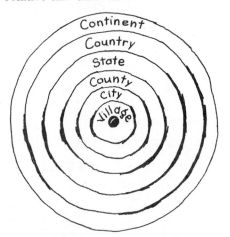

You can show the child the same idea by drawing concentric circles and labeling the different circles. Later draw concentric circles and ask the child to label them. Instead of general geographical terms, a child can use specific place names—where he lives, where his grandparents live, etc.

11. Take a Styrofoam ball. Have the child cut out traced sketches of continents. Ask her to put them in the proper place on the Styrofoam ball which represents a globe.

12. Have the child shape countries or continents out of pipe cleaners.

13. Have the child draw a map of his route to school.

14. For long-term map work, paste the map you are using on a file folder and cover it on both sides with clear Contact paper. You can use all types of maps and practice a variety of skills:

    Measuring the distance between two places, using the key or legend
    Matching countries to continents
    Finding state capitals in the United States

    (You can write on these maps with a magic marker; marks can be erased with a damp tissue. These maps can be easily stored and reused.)[2]

15. Using a map of the United States, with a toy plane and a toy car, play the following game: Map out the route of a trip that will take you from one end of the country to the other, labeling a number of stops. Take turns shaking dice and moving the number of stops called for on the dice. The one who reaches the destination first wins. You may use maps of other countries and continents.

16. For anyone who confuses west and east, put the symbol ←WE→ at the top of the map. The W will help him remember which side is west and the E, which side is east.

17. For map work, use *Map Skills for Today* Series (Xerox Education Publications, Columbus, Ohio 43216) or *Finding Ourselves* (Eileen Lynch Corcoran, Frank E. Richards Publishing Co., Inc., Phoenix, N.Y. 13135).

Time

Time to a little child is the present moment. Ideas of past, present, and future are blurred. The past can be yesterday or early this morning, and the future can be when Daddy comes home or tomorrow.

It is easier for children to learn through concrete experiences, through looking, touching, and feeling. However, they cannot see or touch yesterday or tomorrow, a decade or a century. Because time is abstract, it is difficult to learn.

Time is meaningful to young children only when it relates to their own activities; they have lunch time, nap time, and play time. Relative time is an enigma to them. When mother tells her three-year-old Betsy that

[2]This type of map was devised by Jocelyn Eichler, New Rochelle, N.Y.

she can stay out and play a *little longer* but must come in *soon,* all Betsy understands is that she may continue playing. Betsy in all likelihood will go on playing until doomsday—unless her mother calls her in.

Think of all the units of time a child must learn eventually: *parts of the day*—morning, noon, afternoon; *parts of the night*—evening, night, midnight; *calendar time*—days of the week (7), months of the year (12), seasons of the year (4), days in a month (28, 30, 31), decade (10 years), score (20 years), century (100 years); *clock time*—hour, minute, second.

In the upper grades the student has to learn to place historical time in perspective; he must know when events occurred and relate them to other world events of the same period. Probably he will make timelines and relate time to cause and effect—what happened when and what were the results. For example, to comprehend the civil rights movement in the United States, he must be aware of the causes and results of slavery in colonial times, the Civil War from 1860–1864, and more than 100 years of congressional legislation and Supreme Court rulings pertinent to the movement.

In order to understand units of time in its many aspects, it is obvious that a child needs many different skills. These include sequencing, memory, concept of numbers, and directionality. Weakness in these areas is not unusual for the learning-disabled child. In his early school years, he will need help in remembering and sequencing the days of the week or the months of the year, in counting, in understanding *before* and *after* on the clock and in telling time.

The passage of time is a puzzle to many learning-disabled children, no matter how intelligent they may be. Most eight- or nine-year-olds have developed a good idea of time, but not ten-year-old Mary. Her idea of time, like that of a very young child, was *now, this moment.* Moreover, her inability to look ahead, combined with her distractibility, kept her from adhering to any time schedule. Mary's poor time concepts resulted in numerous problems. She was generally late; she could not pace herself to hurry at home and in school, and was irritated and anxious by the pressure of time in both places. She had no idea what to do in her free time.

Reversing the concepts of time the way they do letters is another failing of some learning-disabled children. For example, Fred, age eight, proudly said, "I'm going to the World Series the day before tomorrow." Another problem plaguing these children is their difficulty in dealing with anything in reverse order. They are perplexed by a story that goes from the present to the past and by television programs that use flashback techniques. A high school student with residual learning problems may still have trouble knowing which month comes before September, and to recall this, must start at the beginning of the year and work his way forward, month by month, from January to August.

All children develop slowly in their ability to put time in proper perspective, but children hampered by learning problems take an unusually long time to achieve this. When children regard their parents as ancient, we are not surprised when they put their grandparents in the same era as George Washington. They are unable to put people and events in the proper historical slots and cannot conceive of the chronological passage of time—history as we know it.

A Sense of Time

Nearly everything we do in life is timed, and we all abide by the same clock time, whether we use a Mickey Mouse watch or a quartz clock. Our individual sense of time, however, is regulated by our own inner clocks. Just as we have our individual thermostats that control our individual temperatures, we contain our inner clocks that fix our individual time sense. Inner clocks can be slow or fast like their real models, and consequently, people differ greatly in their sense of time, regardless of intelligence. Some people feel very strongly about being on time; others do not mind being late unless they have an appointment they consider important. At the airport, some people will check in way ahead of schedule; others will scurry in just as the gates are closing.

The sense of time is an important trait of personality and has serious implications for education. The child who can adjust quickly to new situations and to different methods of teaching is an easy child for the parent and an easy student for the teacher. The child who takes too much time to adjust to new situations and to do his homework has to be handled carefully. He cannot be pushed or he will become anxious and work even more slowly or not at all. With encouragement and supportive guidance, he will gradually quicken his pace and learn to manage time better. Conversely, there are many anxious children who rush everything they do. They are speed demons, not stopping to think before they speak, read, or write; they need to be slowed down. Both the extremely slow-paced children and the hyperactive children who cannot be slowed down need specific help and sometimes a special school.

TIME DEVELOPMENTAL TIMETABLE

A four-to-five-year-old is expected:
- to identify pictures of winter and summer.
- to know why we need clocks.
- to know his age.

A five-to-six-year-old is expected:
- to be able to name the days of the week.
- to know his birthday and how old he will be on his next birthday.
- to have some understanding of tomorrow and yesterday.
- to know morning and afternoon.

A seven-to-eight-year-old is expected:
- to tell time. However, he is still dependent on someone else to tell him what he should be doing at a particular time.
- to know what season it is.
- to know what month it is. By eight, he can name the months in order.

An eight-to-ten-year-old is expected:
- to have developed a realistic sense of time. Some may use their watches just for telling time; others, for being on time.
- to get himself to school on time.
- to follow a school schedule.
- to take an active part in planning his activities.
- to be more aware of the meaning of historical time. For example, Columbus discovered America before the Pilgrims landed at Plymouth Rock.

Activities to Improve the Concept of Time

For the very young child

1. Show him photographs of himself when he was a baby, and pictures of his parents and grandparents taken at different ages.

2. Tell stories about when his grandmother and grandfather were young.

3. Make a pictorial chart of his meals and relate them to different parts of the day.

For the youngster at school

1. Collect pictures of different seasons of the year.

2. Make a calendar with a child and have him mark off each day, so he learns the day and the date.

3. Illustrate the months of the year with meaningful symbols. This is quite helpful for all ages.

Sample from Younger Child   Sample from Older Child

JAN.

FEB.

JAN.

FEB.

4. Have the child make a card for each month of the year. Have him practice arranging them in order, then repeating them in order.

5. Visit museums which have exhibitions of furniture, costumes, transportation, etc. illustrative of different periods of time.

6. Take trips to restored villages, when practical.

7. Collect pictures of the past.

8. Have the child make a timeline of his life from birth to the present.

```
                          Years
                          - 10 -
                          - 9 -  went to camp
                          - 8 -
                          - 7 -
            learned to - 6 -
            ride bike
                          - 5 -  lost first tooth
                          - 4 -
                          - 3 -  fell down steps
                          - 2 -  had 3 stitches
        learned to walk - 1 -
```

9. Make a pictorial timeline. For example, *Land Transportation:* covered wagon; pony express; railroad—coal, steam; cars.

10. Humanize people and periods of history by having children act out creative historical skits.

11. Play the game "Who Am I?" with historical characters studied in school.

12. Explain the meaning of present, past, and future. Put the heading *Present* on a paper. Ask the youngster to list events that he is involved in at the moment. Do this with events that have happened in the *Past* and will happen in the *Future.*

13. Ask the youngster to complete sentences involving time:

> *In the past . . .*
> *On my next birthday . . .*
> *Next summer . . .*
> *Soon . . .*
> *In the future . . .*
> *Two months ago . . .*
> *(If he is studying American history) During colonial times . . .*

14. Clock time (steps toward helping a child to tell time):

a. Be sure the child can count—both forward and backward, in proper sequence. For practice counting forward, have the child write the number which comes after 3 _____, 8 _____, 9 _____, 7 _____. Or ask her to write the number which comes between 1 _____ 3, 5 _____ 7, 10 _____ 12. For practice counting backward, have the child write the number which comes before _____ 4, _____ 6, _____ 8, _____ 12. Or have him pretend he is counting down for the launching of a rocket (10, 9, 8, 7, 6, 5, 4, 3, 2, 1).

b. Show the child the face of a clock. Explain that the little hand represents the hour and the big hand, the minutes. Show him that both hands move to the right. A large cardboard clock is useful for this purpose.

c. Have the child practice telling time on the hour, then the half hour. Have him make his own clock out of a paper plate, cardboard hands, and a paper fastener. After he has put the numbers in the proper place, ask him to show you:
  • What time he gets up in the morning (e.g., 7:00 A.M.)
  • What time he eats lunch (e.g., 12:30 P.M.)
  • What time he goes to bed (e.g., 8:00 P.M.)

d. Explain to the child that 1 hour = 60 minutes, ½ hour = 30 minutes. For practice toward telling time in minutes, learning to count by fives is easy and helpful.

e. Practice telling time by minutes, both *before* and *after* the hour. This is difficult for many children and especially for learning-disabled children.

• Shading half the clock helps them see the difference between *before* and *after:*

• Drawing arrows of different colors indicating *before* and *after* is helpful.

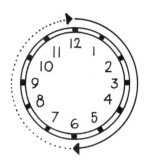

- Drawing lines across the clockface, from 11 to 1, 10 to 2, and so on may help the child see that when the minute hand is at 11, it is 5 *minutes before* the hour; at 1, it is 5 *minutes after* the hour. When the minute hand is at 10, it is *10 minutes before* the hour; at 2, it is *10 minutes after* the hour; and so on. Point out that the numbers opposite each other horizontally on the clock are the same number of minutes away from 12, before and after. (This technique may be particularly helpful to the child who has difficulty counting backwards.)

15. For further practice with clock time and calendar time, use *Learning About Time*, Frank E. Richards Publishing Co., Inc., Phoenix, N.Y. 13135.

LANGUAGE

What level of understanding must a child attain before he is ready for first grade? As language is our primary tool for thinking, well-developed language skills are a prerequisite for school readiness and school learning. The child must understand what other people are saying and must be able to follow oral directions (receptive language). Furthermore, he must be able to express his wants or ideas in simple, well-ordered sentences (expressive language). In other words, he has to understand what he hears and be able to make others understand what he says. His thinking apparatus must be working for both input and output. The average child has a built-in aptitude for language. It is nothing short of a miracle how well a three-year-old has acquired syntax because of an "innate language facility,"[3] and how clearly the average four-year-old speaks.

The role of the mother or mother substitute is vital to the development of a baby's language. The mother who talks to her child stimulates him and, by giving him the necessary feedback, teaches him to communicate. The normal child will follow sequential steps in associating words with meaning and in acquiring concepts, provided that as a baby he has not been deprived of this warm, giving relationship.

From eighteen months to about three years a child's speech is generally egocentric. His mental processes are concerned with satisfying his needs. Gradually he becomes a social being who starts to think about objects and people who are unrelated to his needs. Listening to a child talk will give you a clue to the development of his thinking process—how he associates words with meaning. Suppose a child is asked the question, "What is water?" A three-to-five-year-old might answer "Water is something you drink." A five-to-six-year-old is more descriptive: "Water comes out of a faucet; you drink water; you wash with water, take a bath in it." A six-to-eight-year-old might say "Water is wet" or "Water is a liquid." A junior or senior high school student may tell you that water is a chemical compound, H_2O.

Between two and three, and sometimes earlier, a child will speak in short sentences, and make himself understood. Before you know it, he is telling stories, asking questions, and using complex sentences correctly. The age at which a child starts to speak in sentences can vary. However, if by the age of three, a child does not put two or three words together in sentence form, it would be wise for the parent to find a speech and hearing clinic or to consult a speech pathologist.

It is equally important to seek professional help if the child continues to have immature speech and articulation problems. Certain mispronunciations of letters are acceptable until six or seven; others are not. A first-grade teacher might expect some of her little pupils not to pronounce their *l*'s and *r*'s correctly, for example, but is concerned if they cannot say their *b*'s and *t*'s.

We said that the average child has a built-in aptitude for language. Not so the learning-disabled child. Elements of language, listening, speaking, reading, and writing may be difficult for him. He can have a problem in just one area, or a combination of problems in different areas.

Many learning-disabled children have trouble understanding the

[3]See Noam Chomsky, *Aspects of Theory of Syntax* (Cambridge, Mass.: M.I.T. Press, 1965). Copyright 1965 by The Massachusetts Institute of Technology.

meanings of words, phrases, and sentences. They are frequently unaware that a word can have more than one meaning. When Billy was asked the name of our country, he responded, "Central Park." At twelve, Billy was too old to confuse our country with the woods the way a six-year-old might. Other children with severe language disorders cannot recall the names of objects or people. They tend to give definitions when they are at a loss for a word. Not remembering the word *blackboard,* Susie would talk about "something black that you can write on." Likewise, language-disabled children often remain as literal as preschoolers. Cindy, a fourth-grader, envisioned a real explosion when her mother exclaimed, "My head's about to burst."

Another serious obstacle is the inability to cope with syntax; this often remains a complete mystery to them. Intelligent, eleven-year-old Harry, who had a language disorder, could construct a complicated model car on his own. He once said, "The boys *runned* down the street." "Harry," asked his teacher, "which sentence sounds better—'The boys ran down the road' or 'The boys runned down the road'?" "Sounds the same to me," answered Harry. "I *heared* them the same."

Harry's well-educated parents could not understand the reason for his poor language skills. He had been exposed to proper usage since babyhood. Harry's mother and father had to learn that children with language disabilities do not learn syntax the way average children do; nor do they learn from listening to good models. They have difficulty receiving and processing all types of language. Harry's parents also discovered that Harry had difficulty understanding sentences in the passive tense. He had to think a long time before he could answer the question, "If Captain John Smith was saved by Pocahontas, was Pocahontas saved?" In addition, confused by family relationships, he could not give another name for his mother's sister Sue (aunt) or another name for his mother's mother (grandmother).[4] Difficulties in these areas are not unusual for learning-disabled children, who generally need intensive individual help in all aspects of language.

DEVELOPMENTAL TIMETABLE
IN LANGUAGE AND THINKING

In most children, there is a rapid progression of levels in language and thought development.

A two-to-four-year-old learns to associate a word with its meaning. At a very young age, he can name familiar objects—cup, ball, car.

A three-to-four-year-old connects an object with its use—spoon with eating, glass with drinking.

[4]Elizabeth H. Wiig and Eleanor Messing Semel, *Language Disabilities in Children and Adolescents* (Columbus, Ohio: Charles E. Merrill Publishing Company), p. 113, test items 1 and 5.

A four-to-five-year-old distinguishes things that are alike and different. He can
pick out spoons from forks. Also, in a group of four pictures, he can identify
two that are alike and two that are different.
A five-to-six-year-old can group a number of objects that are alike. He can
separate a pile of paper clips, rubber bands, and erasers into individual
piles of clips, bands, and erasers.
A five-to-six-year-old can generalize or categorize. Given a pencil, crayon, and
chalk, a child at this age can tell you that they are things you write with. He
knows that a peanut-butter sandwich, an orange, and cookies are food.

Abstract Thinking

Generalizing. We have to learn to generalize on many levels. A young child
can tell you that apples and bananas are fruit, but it takes more mature
thinking to tell you that joy and sorrow are both feelings. The ability to
generalize is necessary for abstract thinking, which is related to all academic learning. When we generalize, we must see the relationship of the
parts to the whole and must not see things in isolation.

Making Analogies. Making analogies involves seeing similarities,
differences, and relationships among objects and people. Analogies can
range from the simple to the complex. A five-to-six-year-old might be asked
to complete the sentence: A dog walks; a bird ———— (flies). As a youngster progresses through school, he will have more difficult analogies to
make:

bat *is to* baseball *as* racquet *is to* tennis.
snow *is to* blizzard *as* wind *is to* cyclone.

A high school student might be faced with the following analogy:

taciturn *is to* verbose *as* concise *is to* redundant.

Understanding. A five-to-six-year-old begins to understand abstract
words related to size, time, and space: large, thin, tomorrow, shortly,
beside, behind. (This was discussed earlier in the chapter.) In the upper
elementary years, he comprehends words such as anger, despair,
gratitude. In junior and senior high school, he must be able to define words
that are even more abstract, such as liberty, democracy, justice.

Understanding Different Connotations of Words. Early in his school
years a child must realize that words have different meanings and that the
same word can be used as different parts of speech. Take the word *fair*. As
an adjective, it can mean (1) light in color or blonde, (2) without blemish,
attractive, (3) just and honest, (4) neither very good nor very bad. As a
noun, it means a public place where goods are bought and sold. As another
example, take the word *toll*. As a noun, it can mean (1) a charge made for
the use of a road or bridge, (2) a number lost or killed in battle, (3) deep
notes sounded by a large bell. As a verb, it means to produce deep notes.

Figurative Language (Colloquialisms, Similes, Metaphors, Prov-

64

erbs). Figurative language can be found in all phases of speaking and writing. It allows the speaker or writer to express himself in a vital, colorful, and effective manner. Colloquialisms (familiar sayings) are part of our everyday speech. A child begins using them in elementary school:

> *"I always seem to put my foot in my mouth."*
> *"I'm up to my neck in homework."*

At the same time, children are being introduced to similes (comparisons using *like* or *as*):

> *She was as quiet as a mouse.*
> *He was as sly as a fox.*
> *He slept like a log.*

As a child goes on through school, he will also encounter metaphors (comparisons that are just suggested, in which the words *like* and *as* are omitted):

> *The rain danced on the roof.*
> *He walked on a carpet of colored leaves.*

In junior and senior high school metaphors become more difficult. History texts will refer to expressions such as *seeds of the revolution, The New Deal, The Iron Curtain.* Literature also abounds in metaphors:

> *"The fault, dear Brutus, is not in our stars,*
>   *But in ourselves, that we are underlings."*
>
> (FROM SHAKESPEARE, *JULIUS CAESAR*)
>
> *"Season of mists and mellow fruitfulness,*
>   *Close bosom-friend of the maturing sun"*
>
> (FROM KEATS, *ON AUTUMN*)

At a higher level, a student analyzes proverbs:

> *"Procrastination is the thief of time."*
> *"The pen is mightier than the sword."*

Techniques to Improve Language and Thinking Skills

Grouping: readiness for categorizing

1. After dishes are washed, have a child sort the cutlery into piles of forks, knives, and spoons. Away from home, this can be done with plastic or toy forks, knives, and spoons.

2. After marketing, have a child help unpack the groceries and put them into separate groups—canned goods, boxed goods, bottles.

3. Have a child help sort laundry into piles of similar items—socks, T-shirts, shorts, etc.

4. Give a child a box containing chalk, crayons, and pencils. Ask him to sort them.

5. Give a child a carton of blocks of different sizes, colors, and shapes. Have him sort them by size, color, or shape.

Generalizing: categorizing

1. Place an apple, potato, orange, carrot, cucumber, and banana in a basket or dish. Ask the child to divide them into *fruits* and *vegetables*. A plastic set of fruits and vegetables can also be used.

2. Put rings, pennies, earrings, nickels, bracelets, dimes, necklaces, and quarters on a tray. Ask the child to divide them into two piles, distinguishing between *jewelry* and *coins*. Be sure the child learns these general terms.

3. Ask the child to go through different magazines and find pictures that belong under the following headings:

   Sports
   Transportation
   Furniture
   Buildings
   Tools

4. Cut out different pictures of all types of animals and ask the child to sort them according to those that are *wild* and those that are *domestic or tame*.

5. Ask the child to name:
   different places in which to live (house, motel, tent, trailer)
   different things made of plastic (bottles, toys, trays)
   different things to drink (orange juice, milk, coke)

6. Present the child with an incomplete sentence. Ask her to fill in the missing word—the generalizations:
   Robin, cardinal, bluejay are all _____ (birds).
   Hammer, saw, screwdriver are all _____ (tools).
   Rose, daffodil, tulip are all _____ (flowers).

7. Use *Word-Analysis Practice*, Intermediate Series (Levels A, B, & C), by Donald D. Durrell, Helen A. Murphy, Doris U. Spencer and Jane H. Catterson, Harcourt, Brace & World, Inc., New York, N.Y. (Levels A, B, & C consist of thirty cards each; a student must read the words on a card and decide under which of three suggested categories to write them.)

8. At a higher level, present the student with an incomplete sentence. Ask him to fill in the blank, make the generalization:

   Joy, sorrow, anger, pity are all _____ (feelings).

   Fiction, drama, poetry are all types of _____ (literature).

   Stealing, murder, bribery are all _____ (crimes).

   In all these exercises be sure to reinforce the general terms you are teaching by using different exercises. (For example—Give three other feelings in addition to joy, sorrow, anger, pity.)

Making analogies

Many different types of analogies can be made. The following are examples which you can discuss and use as models.

GRADES 1–3 (APPROXIMATELY)

1. Ask the child to complete the sentence (opposite analogies):

   A bird chirps; a dog _____ (barks).

   A boat sails; an airplane _____ (flies).

   A light shines; a horn _____ (honks, toots).

2. Ask the child to circle the word that would complete the sentence (the analogy):

   Baby is to *man* as *colt* is to _____ (tree, *horse*, girl).

GRADES 3–6 (APPROXIMATELY)

1. Ask the child to make the analogy:

   Step is to *ladder* as *drawer* is to _____ (bureau).

   Beautiful is to *ugly* as *right* is to _____ (wrong).

   Pebble is to *rock* as *twig* is to _____ (branch).

   Calendar is to *time* as *speedometer* is to _____ (distance).

2. You may furnish the children with a word box from which they can find the answers. Put more words in the word box than are needed.

   distance   floor   ruler

   branch   bureau   wrong

GRADES 7–12

   There are many kinds of relationships that can be made between words. Some examples follow. Use them as models:

   Worker and his product—sculptor: statue, tailor: clothes

   Worker and tool—surgeon: scalpel, draftsman: ruler

   Time—dawn: twilight, decade: century

Cause and effect—germ: disease, success: joy
Variations of intensity—large: immense, tepid: hot
Categories—lizard: reptile, spaniel: canine
Synonyms—strange: peculiar, surprise: astonish
Antonyms—comfortable: miserable, wealth: poverty
Part to whole—student: class, bee: swarm

Older students who need practice making analogies should refer to
S.A.T. review books.

Abstract words

From the earliest years through high school, abstract nouns can best
be taught through concrete experiences and discussion.

1. Ask the child to cut out pictures that depict feelings: happiness, sadness,
   fear, or worry. Talk about feelings.

2. Ask the child to draw her own pictures expressing different feelings.
   Have the child describe the picture in her own words. Use her pictures
   to discuss why a person is sad, happy, frightened, anxious, or shy.

3. Use puppets to act out different feelings, such as joy or excitement, or to
   show the meaning of abstract words, such as safety, health, or danger.

4. Collect different pictures illustrating abstract nouns. Ask the child if he
   can guess what the noun in the picture is.

5. Ask the child to make up a story that uses words such as obedience,
   caution, pleasure.

Different connotations of words

Vocabulary building is an important component of reading comprehension. At an early age children should be made aware that words have
different meanings—connotations.

1. A rudimentary way is to use pictures. For example, show the child a
   picture of a cow's horn and a bicycle horn. Ask him to select the picture
   that illustrates the underlined word: His new <u>horn</u> made a loud noise.

2. Ask the child some riddles:
   *What did the tablecloth say to the table? (Don't make a move—I've
   got you covered.)*
   Why did the girl hold on to her nose? (Because it was running.)

3. Ask the child to explain puns—plays on words.
   *Did you hear that the girl threw the clock out of the window because
   she wanted to see time fly?*
   *Did you hear the big firecracker say to the little firecracker, "My pop
   is bigger than your pop?"*

4. Play charades. Act out a word in at least two ways. After the child guesses the word, have him use it in sentences showing different meanings. (Bank, dart, hands, mean, plot, letter are examples of words to use.) Have the child act out a word; try to guess it.

5. Use a word in a sentence. Ask the child to select the correct meaning from different definitions of the word.

Three *times* four make twelve.(2)

There were bad *times* after the flood.(3)

At *times* I'm in a bad mood.(1)

   (1) Sometimes, on occasion

   (2) Multiplied by

   (3) Period marked by conditions

I will be *back* in half an hour.(2)

Jimmy walked to the *back* of the room.(1)

The soccer player is wearing number 9 on his *back*.(3)

   (1) At the rear of

   (2) (to) return

   (3) part of one's body

Figurative language

Discuss figurative language with the children so that they can understand what is meant.

1. Ask the child to complete the following phrases (similes):

red as _____ (a beet, lips, an apple)

sly as a _____ (fox)

straight as _____ (an arrow)

flat as _____ (a pancake)

2. Ask the child to complete the sentences:

The children climbed the trees like _____ (monkeys)

He is so clumsy he dances like _____ (an elephant)

At night the illuminated bridge looks like _____ (a diamond necklace)

3. Give a student a sentence with a metaphor. Ask him to identify what things are being compared and how they are alike:

The birds formed a choir in the apple trees. (Birds and choir are being compared. They are alike because birds sing and members of a choir sing.)

The swallows were dive-bombing over the roof. (Swallows and airplanes are being compared. This particular bird swoops down like a particular plane, a dive bomber.)

4. Titles of old and new songs are a good way of introducing metaphors:

   "You Ain't Nothing but a Hound Dog"

   "I'm Gonna Wash That Man Right Out of My Hair"

   "I'm Sitting On Top of the World"

   "Diamonds Are a Girl's Best Friend"

   "Bridge Over Troubled Water"

5. Discuss familiar sayings with the child:

   Face the music

   Feather in one's cap

   Dead as a doornail

   Take the bull by the horns

   Don't upset the applecart

   Apple of one's eye

   White elephant

   Like a fish out of water

6. Ask the child to match a proverb with a different proverb with similar meaning:

   a. A man is known by the company he keeps.

   b. Don't judge a book by its cover.

   c. Slow and steady wins the race.

   (b) Clothes do not make the man.

   (a) Birds of a feather flock together.

   (c) Little strokes fell great oaks.

In this chapter we have presented the ordered structure of language and conceptual development ranging from the young child to the college student and described sequential steps in teaching language and thinking skills. Referring to developmental stages in this and other areas should help determine what is the appropriate teaching level for an individual.

A list of workbooks and materials pertaining to thinking and language skills can be found at the end of Chapter 6.

5 LEARNING TO READ

If you happen to visit a third-grade class, you may notice that the children are divided into reading groups. The "Helicopters" may be reading a beginning second-grade book; the "Jets" may be reading a third-grade reader; and the "Rockets" could be reading books written on the fourth-grade level and up. Variations in reading abilities can be found in all grades.

Throughout the school years the range of reading abilities will depend largely on how well students have mastered the mechanical aspects (recognizing and deciphering words) and on how well they have developed language and thinking skills. None of these skills, however, operates in a vacuum, and all of them must be integrated. Think of the numerous perceptual and conceptual skills a child must put in his mental Mixmaster in order to read.

A few exceptional children miraculously can read any book by first grade. Most children, however, have to be taught to read. Naturally, their concentration and motivation clearly affect their progress in this area, as does the quality of teaching. Many children learn to read with comparative ease; others find reading hard work, and children with specific learning problems find it a real struggle. Because reading is the primary tool for all school learning, a handicap in this area can be painful, long-lasting, and destructive to a child's self-image.

Most parents are not unduly concerned if their son walks a little later than his cousin, Joe, or if Mary's first molar makes its debut later than expected. But they tend to become extremely anxious if their son or daughter does not start to read in first grade. The nonreading child senses when his parents are disappointed, which adds to his frustration. This situation may be even more difficult if, by chance, he has an older sister or brother who excelled in reading in first grade.

Everyone does not have to read at a college level. Nevertheless, a person must have fairly good reading skills for all school learning and for adult living. In addition, children should discover that reading is not just a means to an end, but an end in itself; they should experience the joy and fun in reading. Not only is reading a pleasurable activity for leisure time, it is a pathway to new horizons—to unfamiliar people, places, and ideas. As Herbert Spencer, the writer, said, "Reading is seeing by proxy."

In all learning, there are generally sequential steps of development. Reading is no exception. Although children show marked differences in the rate at which they acquire reading skills, eventually they all have to master the same steps. Some children may skim rapidly through certain stages but may progress more slowly in others. Jimmy breezed through the mechanics of reading, but was much slower in developing comprehension skills. In contrast, Sally struggled with the mechanics, but did extremely well when the emphasis was on comprehension.

Most reading problems for learning-disabled children, as well as problems in other subjects, stem from gaps in various stages of academic development. These gaps become their learning disabilities. With appropriate help students can fill these voids or learn to compensate for their problems.

Remedial programs are vitally important. Such programs require additional personnel and materials, and this poses problems for schools serving poor neighborhoods. However, many of these areas have benefitted from programs financed through Title I of the Elementary and Secondary Education Act of 1965. It provides the neediest children with remedial training in basic skills, especially reading. Recently, there has been a breakthrough for remedial education. Schools have now shown that compensatory teaching can be successful. The National Assessment of Educational Progress reported in April 1981 that nationwide gains in reading in the 1970's can be attributed to remedial education.

STAGES OF READING: PRESCHOOL DEVELOPMENT AND FUTURE ACADEMIC EXPECTATIONS

First Stage: Preschool–1st Grade

Reading readiness

1. Recognizing pictures of familiar objects in a book: A child links a printed word with a spoken word which is the name of a familiar object.

2. Recognizing words from a sign—STOP—after hearing an adult say the word as he points to the sign. He can select a package of PIZZA from the grocery shelf on seeing the illustration.

3. Taking cues from the shape and size of words on the title: A three-year-old will mystify his parents when he selects records he wants to play and tells them, "This is *Jack and Jill*" or "This is *Farmer in the Dell.*"

4. Learning words from the television screen and from advertisements.

5. Developing perceptual and conceptual skills in kindergarten and first grade. Being able to discriminate letter forms and letter sounds. (See Chapters 3 and 4.)

Second Stage:
1st Grade–4th Grade

Mechanics of reading: main focus of instruction

1. Learning the sounds of letters and letter combinations.

2. Combining letters and their sounds to form words (blending).

3. Developing a basic sight vocabulary.

4. Learning basic rules which help a child sound out words—for example, the "silent *e*" rule.

5. Tackling compound words: pan/cake, fire/man.

6. Learning word parts: roots, prefixes, suffixes, and syllabication.

7. Practicing oral reading:
   to reinforce word attack skills
   to help children overcome problems of omissions, additions, and substitutions of words and word parts, which are fairly common in these grades
   to learn to stress words correctly and to recognize punctuation
   to improve pronunciation and expression

Introduction of elementary comprehension skills

Building comprehension skills by reading stories and simple factual material, followed by asking children relevant questions.
   A few sample questions:

What is the story about?
Who was the main character?
What happened first? Next? Last?
Where did the story take place?

Third Stage:
4th Grade Up

Comprehension: focus of reading instruction

1. Understanding words and building vocabulary

2. Understanding sentences, sentence structure, and syntax

3. Understanding paragraphs

   Finding the main thought and the topic sentence
   Finding important details
   Drawing conclusions and interpreting what you read

Phonics: refining word attack skills

Silent reading and rate of reading

MECHANICS OF READING:
HOW CHILDREN ARE TAUGHT

Children are taught to read by a combination of methods depending on a school's orientation. Over the years, the teaching of reading has been a controversial subject. The pendulum has swung back and forth between the pure *look-say* and pure *phonics* approaches. To meet the needs of more children, modern methods include the best aspects of both, combined with linguistic systems which focus on the spelling patterns of words—word families such as pin, tin, win. For a time, there was a surge of new and revised reading programs offered to schools and teachers. Each of these programs was claimed to be *the* method for teaching reading and over-coming problems. Today, educators are aware that there is no one method; different children need different systems. A good teacher, given the re-sources and a flexible situation, will use varied reading programs. In this way, she will help more children by selecting the methods that best suit particular learning styles. It is especially important to find the appropriate methods for the learning-disabled child. In recent years, reading specialists have developed diagnostic-prescriptive methods for students needing remedial help. It is interesting to note that in a number of schools this type of analysis is now used for teaching all students.

Although the average child entering kindergarten or first grade has a large speaking vocabulary, he can identify only a limited number of written words, which he has picked up from television programs, signs, the super-market, etc. In the beginning of the school year, a teacher may label objects in the classroom: door, paper, crayons, paints, closet, etc. Later on, she will see if the children can label these objects on their own. To help a child learn new words, she will generally start teaching her class sight words through meaningful experience stories. For example:

A Walk

We went for a walk around the school.
We saw the sixth grade.
We saw the nurse.
We saw the gym.
We saw the auditorium.
We saw the lost and found room.

She will choose a few words from the story, put them on cards and match them to words in the story as she says them. She will then ask the children to do the same thing. These words will become part of their sight word vocabulary.

Children learn more easily from what is meaningful for them—no matter where they live or what their background is. An outstanding example of this was Sylvia Ashton-Warner's teaching of the Maori and white children in a provincial New Zealand school. She taught them reading through their own vocabulary and experiences. One child, Rongo, wrote:

Mummy is crying
because Daddy
hit her in the face. Mummy is
going to Nanny's today. Daddy is
angry.
just because
Daddy got wild
and so I got
wild because
Daddy was drunk.
Then he hit
Rongo.[1]

Kent would have done very well in Mrs. Ashton-Warner's class. He certainly did not make progress in the first, second, and third grades in his local school. No one knew what to do with Kent; he just could not learn to read. Even the reading teacher was puzzled. Because Kent was artistic, his classroom teacher thought he would be happier spending the reading period in the art room. Finally his parents had him tested outside of school. Diagnosis showed that his memory, both auditory and visual, was weak. He had not learned all his sounds and knew very few sight words. It was recommended that Kent be tutored individually by a warm, competent learning disabilities specialist.

Discovering that Kent's main interest in life was nature, his tutor had him dictate stories to her about birds, caterpillars, and squirrels. From

[1]Sylvia Ashton-Warner, *Teacher* (New York: Bantam Books, Inc., 1964), p. 152. Copyright © 1963 by Sylvia Ashton-Warner. Reprinted by permission of Simon & Schuster, a Division of Gulf & Western Corporation.

these stories he learned many new words. Using these words, she taught him phonics. For example, from cardinal, cocoon, and caterpillar, he learned one sound for *c*. She used the sound of *ar* in cardinal to teach the sound of *ar*. Until Kent acquired more basic skills, his tutor devised as many techniques as possible built upon his interests. One of the lessons designed to improve visual discrimination involved working with a collection of sea shells. In this activity, which he enjoyed, he was asked to match shells to pictures in a shell book. At the same time he learned to read the words labeling the shells.

Kent had a desire to learn to read, but reading was a struggle. Undoubtedly, the teaching techniques based largely on his interests helped him cope. After several years of tutoring, he made substantial progress.

Look-Say Approach

The *look-say* method is a visual approach to reading whereby a child learns to recognize a word as a whole. A teacher introduces one word at a time, by writing a word on the board or a card and saying it. She will have the child say it as he looks at it; then she will ask him to close his eyes and try to visualize it in his mind. Finally he will repeat it. She will use these words repeatedly in stories, captions, and exercises until they are learned. The child will build up a large sight vocabulary which he will recognize and practice in his school readers.

Through the *look-say* method, a child's sight vocabulary can become the basis for learning sounds. He must eventually learn letter sounds, because he cannot memorize the whole English language and needs to be able to sound out unknown words. Basically, after a child has learned a group of words beginning with the same sound—*boat, best, bus, bat*—he will associate the letter which begins these words with its sound, the sound of *b* in this case. From another group of words, *fire, foot, fan, fit*, he will pick up the sound of *f*—and so on. This method of learning sounds indirectly through sight words is particularly good for the youngster with a *strong visual memory* but a *weak auditory memory*.

It must be remembered that no matter by which method a child is learning to read, he will have to identify certain words by sight—words that can not be broken down into phonetic elements, such as *buy*.

Techniques for Learning Sight Words

1. Write the word on the blackboard or a card. Say it as you write it. Have the child repeat it while looking at it. Ask him to close his eyes and picture it, and then to open his eyes and repeat it.

2. Paste a picture (from catalogues, magazines, or coloring books) on a card. Print the word under the picture. On the other side of the card,

write just the word. Practice doing this with different words he is learning until he does not need the picture clue to know the word.

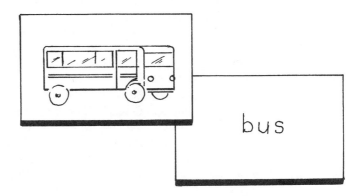

3. After the child knows some words, use them in exercises. Ask the child to choose the word that makes sense in the sentence:

The boy _____*(sees)*_____ *the train.*
      (fly, sees)

The girl _____*(jumps)*_____ *rope.*
      (jumps, run)

4. Have the child (or student) keep a box of sight word cards. Review them periodically with him. Put a check on each card every time he knows that word. After reading any word or words correctly four or five times, a child may happily tear up the card or file it away.

5. Draw a baseball diamond. Using a child's sight word cards and two small figures, play the "game" of baseball. Every time the child gets one of his words correct, he advances a base, and eventually he scores runs. Should he make a mistake, his opponent advances a base.

6. Make a bingo grid of sight words and play bingo with the words a child needs to practice recognizing.

7. Commercial materials that are available:
   Vocabulary Cards, E.W. Dolch, Garrard Publishing Co., Champaign, Ill.
   Sight Phrase Cards, E.W. Dolch, Garrard Publishing Co., Champaign, Ill.
   Grab (Junior and Senior Deck), Dorothy Alcock, Inc., Covina, Ca. (Available in four levels of difficulty.)

8. Have a child make up and dictate a story using words she is learning.

The Phonics Approach

The phonics method is an auditory approach. The child has to learn to associate a letter directly with its sound, and letter combinations directly with their sounds.

Once he knows a number of consonant sounds and one or more short vowel sounds, he is ready for blending. This skill requires combining sounds to form words (m-a-p, map). This step can be difficult for many children, but particularly for those who cannot integrate sounds to produce a whole word. For these children, the word-family approach (see p. 86) will help them learn to blend more easily. In addition, in this approach the child will learn certain rules which will help him sound out new words.

To learn by the phonic method, a child must be able to distinguish and remember letter sounds. Learning-disabled children who have a poor visual memory, but adequate auditory skills, do well with this approach.

BASIC PHONICS NECESSARY FOR READING

Sounds of the single consonants: b, c, d, f, m, n . . .

Long and short sounds of vowels: a, e, i, o, u

Consonant blends: bl, br, cl, cr, dr, st, tr, sp, spr, str . . .

Consonant diagraphs: ch, sh, wh, th, ck . . .

Rules for long sound of vowels

Special vowel sounds: au, aw, o͝o, o͞o, ea, ow, ou, oi, oy (ow, ou, oi, oy referred to as dipthongs)

Sounds of vowels with *r*: ar, er, ir, or, ur

Rules for soft *c* and soft *g*:

1. When *c* is followed by *e, i,* or *y,* it is usually soft; it has the sound of *s, cent, city, cycle.*
2. When *g* is followed by *e, i,* or *y,* it is usually soft; it has the sound of *j, gem, giant, gym.*

Silent letters: *mb* (lamb), *kn* (knife), *gn* (gnat), *wr* (wrong)

Recognition of root words, prefixes, and suffixes

Division of words into syllables

Usually by the end of third grade, but sometimes not until the end of fourth, the above phonics skills are largely mastered. The hierarchy of skills may vary slightly from school to school. One may introduce blends toward the end of first grade; another, not until second grade. One may start with the consonants *m, f, l;* another with *t, m, d, h.* When working with a child on phonics skills, check what he is doing in school and ask to see the materials he is using. From his workbooks, the volunteer teacher or tutor can make sure of the order in which phonics elements are being introduced in the classroom. (For an overview of phonics, see *Phonics in Perspective,* by Arthur W. Heilman, Charles E. Merrill Co., Columbus, Ohio, 1964.)

Techniques to Use
for the Phonics Approach

The following techniques to help a child learn to associate a letter with its sound use the letter *f* as an example. However, the same techniques can be used to teach all letters and letter combinations and their sounds.

1. Hold up a card with the letter *f* on it and give the sound of the letter. Then show a picture of a fish. Tell the child that fish begins with the *f* sound and repeat the *f* sound.

2. Ask the child to look through several magazines and cut out pictures of objects beginning with the sound of *f*. She can make a file of these pictures in alphabetical order or use them in a scrapbook.

3. Put *f* at the top of a page. Ask the child to draw objects beginning with the sound of *f*.

4. Ask the child to name objects beginning with the sound of *f*.

> Teacher: *Look around the room. Can you think of things beginning with the* f *sound?*
> Child: *File, fan, finger.*

Teacher: *Can you think of other things beginning with the sound of f?*

Child: *Fire engine, farm, foot.*

5. Ask the child riddles. His response must begin with the *f* sound.

Teacher: *How did you run when you were late for school?*

Child: *Fast.*

6. Take pictures of foot, fence, fire; ask him to write the letter he hears at the beginning of these words.

7. Have the child write the letter *f* with a felt-tip pen while saying the sound of *f*.

8. To know a letter and its sound for reading, spelling, and writing, a child must be able to make three associations:
   • Say the sound of a letter when he sees the letter.
   • Say the letter when he hears its sound.
   • Write the letter when he hears its sound.

A child must also be able to hear the sound of a letter when it is at the beginning, in the middle, and at the end of words. To practice this you can draw three boxes in a row on the board. Ask the child to write the letter whose sound she hears in different words in the first box if the letter begins the word, in the middle box if its sound is in the middle, in the last box if the sound ends the word. Put *f* where you hear the *f* sound in the following words:

fat	f		
puff			f
muffin		f	

There are many techniques for reinforcing the sounds of letters:

1. From a collection of small toys, take a fork, a top, and a car, whose beginning sounds the child knows. Put them on a piece of paper; have the child write the letter connected with the beginning sound of the names of the toys.

2. Point out that in some letters you can hear their sounds at the beginning of their names: *b, d, j, k, p, t, v, z*. In some letters, you can hear their sounds at the end of their names: *f, l, m, n, s, x*. (Others have their own peculiar sounds: *h, y, w*.)

3. Take folded newspaper or floor tiles; with a magic marker write the letters of the sounds that need reviewing in large print on the newspaper or tiles. Put them on the floor. Ask the child to step on the one whose sound he hears at the beginning of a word you chose to represent that sound.

4. Make a checkerboard of the letters whose sounds you are reviewing and reinforcing. Ask the child to place a large button on the letter whose beginning sound she hears in a word you say.

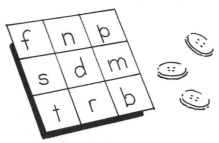

5. Play the game *Go Fish* (produced by the Remedial Education Center, Washington, D.C.) to teach the letters and their sounds. This rummy-type game, in which the players ask for cards by their sounds, is very effective in teaching letter sounds.

6. Play *Consonant Lotto*, E.W. Dolch, Garrard Publishing Co., Champaign, Ill.

Techniques for Teaching Short Vowel Sounds

Short vowels are more difficult letter sounds for everyone to learn. Learning-disabled children may find them a particular stumbling block because their sounds are so similar. The following techniques can be added to the ones already listed for teaching letter sounds.

1. Keep a collection of key words for the short vowel sounds. Have the child refer to a card such as those on page 82 when a particular sound does not come easily.

81

2. Give the child who has difficulty remembering the short sounds of the vowels a memory mark for vowels, which he can keep at the back of his book. This can be made by the teacher or the child.

3. For the older student or adult who still has problems with certain vowel sounds *and* knows too many words by sight, practice will have to be done with nonsense words and syllables.

4. Use the *Short Vowel Drill*, produced by the Remedial Education Center, Washington, D.C.

5. Play *Pound the Sound*. For each vowel, make cards with pictures of objects whose name starts with that vowel. For example, for *a:* ax, apple, astronaut; for *o:* orange, octopus.

    File the cards according to their vowel sounds in a box divided into five sections and labeled *a, e, i, o, u*. The children must be able to sort the cards according to their initial letter sounds before they can play the game. To play the game:

   a. Shuffle the cards.

   b. Choose the sound you want to "pound."

   c. Holding the cards face down, the teacher turns the cards over one at a time.

   d. When the card with the chosen sound appears, the child tries to pound it before the teacher does.

   e. If he pounds the correct sound, he wins the pile; if he pounds the wrong sound, he loses the cards. (The pounding is going to reinforce the sound.)

6. Play the commercial game *Sea of Vowels* (Ideal Toy Co., New York, N.Y.)

7. For vowels, consonants, consonant blends, use *Montessori Matters*, Sisters of Notre Dame de Namur, 701 E. Columbia Ave., Cincinnati, Ohio.

8. Use *Vowel Wheels*, Milton Bradley Company, Springfield, Mass.

Techniques to Help Children Blend

1. Demonstrate blending in a simple way. Take a word like *tap*. Separate it into only two parts, t-ap. Say it for the child in two parts, then say the word as a whole. This will give the child an idea of what is meant by blending.

2. Say a word in all its parts, f-a-n, very slowly, and ask the child if he can guess what the word is. If he can, he is ready for blending.

3. Next take a printed word, *hit*. Show the child how the sounds can be blended together to form a word. Blend very slowly, then faster and faster (h--i--t, h-i-t, hit).

4. Blending is a challenge to most young readers and an obstacle to many learning-disabled children. For those having problems at this point, often the word-family (linguistic) approach is easier.

5. If a child cannot blend fast enough or cannot seem to get the word out, have him hold up a card with a word on it. When he looks at the word, ask him to blow out all the sounds of the letters he sees in one breath—as if he were blowing out a candle.

6. Another technique which may be helpful involves banging toys together. For example, take two little toys (or objects) such as an apple and a nut. Give the child an apple which stands for short *a* and a nut which stands for *n*. Have him bang the two together as he says their sounds, *a-n*, forming the word *an*.

Rules for Teaching
Long Vowel Sounds

1. Silent *e*, or magic *e* rule: An *e* at the end of a word (or syllable) is silent and the vowel before it says its name: bak*e*, tim*e*. The following type of card can be made by the child to practice using the silent *e* rule.

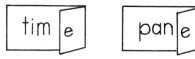

2. When two vowels come together in a word, the second one is usually silent; the first one says its name: rain, boat, feed, team.

For Further Practice in Phonics

1. Use *New Phonetic Word Drill Cards*, Kenworthy Educational Service, Inc., Buffalo, N.Y.

2. *Group Sounding Game*, E.W. Garrard Publishing Co., Champaign, Ill.

3. *Phonics Rummy* (Junior A,B,C), Phono-Visual Products, Kenworthy Educational Services, c/o John Green, Covington, Ky.

Techniques for Seeing and Hearing
Different Parts of Words

Compound words

Help a child recognize that compound words are two words put together. He needs to see and hear the different parts.

pan cake pancake
bat man batman
rain coat raincoat

Have students draw lines between the two shorter words that make compounds: sail/boat, gold/fish.

Put the compound words on cards. Have the student cut the words into their two parts (two shorter words).

Write compound words on separate cards. Cut each word into two parts (two shorter words). Mix them up on the table. Ask the child to put the parts together to form compound words.

As a child learns more difficult sounds, he can tackle more difficult compound words; for example, *barnyard, downpour*.

Root words and common word endings

Explain what a root word is and how it can be changed by adding different endings: *looks, looked, looking. Look* is the root or base word; *s, ed, ing* are the first endings introduced. Later on introduce *er* (slower), *est* (slowest), *ly* (lately), *y* (pesty).

Have the child practice identifying root words by circling the base word of each of the following:

Have the child add correct endings to words. Ask him to fill in the missing parts:

Tom is fish_____. (ing)
Last night Jane call_____ her friend. (ed)
The cat lick_____ the dish as she eats. (s)

Prefixes and suffixes

Explain to the student that prefixes and suffixes are word parts which alter the meanings of words. Prefixes come at the beginning of a word—*un*happy, *re*call—and suffixes at the end—care*ful*, rest*less*.

Have a child draw a circle around the prefix in a word:

Have a child draw a circle around the suffix in a word:

Prefixes, suffixes, and root words are studied in conjunction with vocabulary and comprehension throughout the school years. See Chapter 6.

Dividing words into syllables

Explain to the youngster that every syllable has one vowel sound (either short or long), and that before he can divide words into parts he must recognize what a syllable is.

1. Have him clap or tap as he hears each syllable when you say a word.
2. Have him identify the vowel sound when he reads a word: bat, boat, breathe. Point out that these words have one, two, and three vowels respectively, but that each word has only one vowel *sound;* and therefore all are one-syllable words.

After a youngster is able to identify syllables, teach him some important rules of syllabication.

1. When two consonants come between two vowels in a word, the word divides into syllables between the consonants. (When teaching this rule, start with words which have two consonants that are alike, then move to words in which the consonants are different.)

   pū py   bas ket
   din ner   sub ject
   let ter   wit ness

2. When one consonant comes between two vowels in a word, the word is usually divided into syllables before the consonant, and the vowel is usually long: lā dy, t ī ger, mō tel. Sometimes the word is divided after the consonant, and the vowel has a short sound: trăv el, prĭs on.

3. If a word ends with *le*, the consonant before the *le* joins the *le* to form the last syllable of that word: cra dle, bot tle, crum ble.

Two useful generalizations about vowel sounds taught in conjunction with syllabication:

1. If a syllable ends in a vowel, the vowel is usually long; for example, pō ny, rā dar.

2. If a syllable ends in a consonant, the vowel is usually short; for example, răb bĭt, pĭc nĭc.

Use the same techniques for dividing words into syllables that were illustrated for dividing compound words into parts:

1. Making them: num/ber, ta/ble
2. Physically cutting them into syllables: be gin, lo cate
3. Putting syllable cards together to form words
4. Using a continuing pencil movement to group syllables: num ber

Word-Family Approach

Children who have difficulty blending letters to form words find it easier to learn through the linguistic or word-family approach. If they are able to rhyme, they can be taught new words by adding different consonants to the same word ending. For example, the word *cat* can be changed to *hat, bat, mat* by just substituting another initial consonant. Word families have been used with many different reading programs through the years because of their effectiveness. They are widely used with learning-disabled children who have considerable difficulty in both blending and learning their short vowel sounds. In blending, it is easier to combine an initial consonant and a word-family ending (m-op, h-op, t-op) than to blend single letters into a word (p-o-p). As for short vowel sounds, if a child sees, hears, and writes, for example, *pin, tin, fin,* or *hit, fit, sit,* often enough, the sound of short *i* finally penetrates.

Techniques for Using the Word-Family Approach

1. Write a few rhyming words and underline their endings. Write several similar endings without initial consonants. After reading the first few words to the child, see if he can produce new words by adding consonants at the beginning.

   > p*at*
   > m*at*
   > s*at*
   > (h)*at*
   > (r)*at*

2. Highlight the word family by using a different color to write the word ending.

3. Use *Wooden Block Letters* from Childcraft Equipment Co., Inc., New York, N.Y., *Link Letters,* or *Anagrams,* both from Milton Bradley Company, Springfield, Mass. Put letters together to form a word: *map.* Ask the child to change the beginning consonant to form another word, then another; or have him make several words in the same family: *not, cot.*

4. Have the child make up stories and poems using word families:

   > The top is on the mop.
   > The nut is in the hut.

5. Play commercial games that are available: *Word Family Fun* (Kenworthy Educational Service, Inc., Buffalo, N.Y.) or *Pirate Keys* (Antioch Bookplate Co., Yellow Springs, Ohio).

The Kinesthetic and Tactile Approach

Children with severe reading and spelling disorders often do not respond to methods based on hearing and seeing letters and words. Some of them, however, make progress when techniques involving movement (kinesthetic) and touch (tactile) are introduced. Combining these procedures with auditory and visual techniques results in a multisensory approach which is often quite successful.

Techniques

(Parts of the kinesthetic method which follows were first introduced by Grace Fernald.)

1. Have the child select a word he wants to learn. Write or print it in large letters on a card. Have the child trace it with his finger, saying each part as he does so. He repeats this until he can write the word from memory. Have him file each new word alphabetically in his own file box. Have him use his words in a sentence or story. Type them as soon as possible so he can read them in printed form.

2. Make a letter or word out of window sealer (Mortite). Have the child trace it with his finger. Then have the child trace around it with a pencil. Ask him to say the letter (or word) while tracing. The child can make his own letter or word with Mortite. If he can, have him copy it with a crayon, magic marker, pen, or pencil, whatever he uses best.

3. Additional materials used for making letters and words for the child to touch and trace include sandpaper, pipe cleaners, clay, and Playdoh.

4. For tactile techniques to be effective, a child must have an adequate sense of touch.[2]

Workbooks

Most children learn and reinforce the basic skills through workbooks in school. However, workbooks cannot be used indiscriminately. Choose them carefully. The selection should be based on the approach best suited for a particular child. It must be pointed out that many learning-disabled children are subjected to too many workbooks. For them, interchange workbooks with creative material, such as has been suggested. (Examples of different types of workbooks are listed at the end of the chapter.)

Many workbooks are written to accompany basal readers, which are produced by leading publishers. A Basal Reading program is an organized method of planned instruction. Many teachers base their reading lessons on this type of program. Teachers' manuals which accompany basal readers can be very helpful. It should be noted that basal readers vary in their approach to reading. Some emphasize phonics, others sight words, still others word families. It should also be noted that they can vary in difficulty at the same level. The second-grade reader of one program may be as advanced as the third-grade book of another series.

[2]Adapted from Grace M. Fernald, *Remedial Techniques in Basic School Subjects* (New York: McGraw-Hill Book Company, 1943).

Case Study

The case of eight-year-old Pat, which follows, illustrates *why* certain techniques and books were chosen and used to help a child with learning problems.

Pat was the outstanding athlete in her class. During recess when the boys and girls picked sides for a baseball game, Pat was always chosen first. She was the best batter in the third grade; she was also the worst reader. Her reading problem was beginning to worry Pat, although it did not detract from her popularity. "I'm so good in sports, but so dumb in reading," she would tell her mother. She could read only a few sight words and had difficulty writing. Although she could compute mental math problems quickly, she could not even tackle written problems because of her inability to read. This inability also affected her performance in social studies. Her teacher felt that Pat was extremely intelligent, and praised her verbal expression and class participation. Being the best athlete in the class helped Pat's self-esteem, but she was becoming frustrated and anxious about her school work.

Informal testing spotted many problems. Pat was confused about right and left when she played *Simon Says;* she could not say the months in order; and in telling time, she had trouble recognizing which side of the clock was *before* and which was *after* the hour. She reversed some letters, *d* for *b*, for instance, and in numbers, wrote Γ for 7, and $\mathsf{2}$ for 5. When asked to draw a diamond, she drew one which looked like rabbit ears instead of a figure with angles. Her major area of weakness was auditory. While she knew most of her consonant sounds, she had difficulty blending letter sounds to form a word, even when helped. She did not know any vowels and could not hear the differences in their sounds.

A delightful, attractive child, Pat focused well on all tasks, showed excellent concentration, and made persistent efforts when faced with difficult activities. She talked intelligently and was well informed for her age. Her visual discrimination was good; she could select the proper letter when presented with a group of letters. Her visual memory was strong; through labeling, she was able to learn the words desk, chair, and lamp, and soon after, could read those words on cards. She figured out quickly how many nickels made a dollar, with good reasoning. Moreover, she could remember oral sentences at the thirteen-year level, which was five years ahead of her chronological age. Even though she was worried about her poor school achievement, she was self-motivated and wanted to learn.

Surveying Pat's strengths and weaknesses, the examiner felt that Pat presented the picture of an intelligent, learning-disabled child, who had many strengths combined with some distinct immaturities. A big asset was her ability to concentrate and focus on her work, a characteristic not always found in learning-disabled children.

The learning disabilities specialist gave Pat an understanding of her problems and pointed out that she had great strengths and could overcome her weaknesses with extra help. Pat felt better when her tutor described prominent people who had coped with similar problems.

It was very clear from the evaluation that Pat had not learned to read through the phonics approach, which was the basis of reading instruction in her school. So, knowing that Pat could rhyme, the tutor started teaching her to read through word families. On the board, she listed words that rhymed with *Pat* and had her add words with the same endings. Next she wrote a sentence using three of these words: *Pat sat on a mat.* Pat was delighted that she could read this.

In a short time Pat became familiar with short *a* and short *i* words by doing exercises in the *Primary Phonics* workbook, using link letters and playing word-family games. In addition, she was learning sight words and reinforcing all her work through writing. Soon she was able to read *Pins and Pans*, a Sullivan reader based on the word-family approach. She learned other word families, and gradually learned the short vowel sounds in isolation. At this point, more phonics were introduced. Once she had achieved some success through individual tutoring, she progressed rapidly.

When working with learning-disabled children or adults, one of the tasks is to select the appropriate techniques and reading programs. These may be the same techniques used in regular classrooms in some schools, but the learning-disabled student, like Pat, needs more time, more reinforcement, and more support.

The vital supportive role of a tutor or teacher is described in the following light verse written by a caring volunteer, who worked with young children.

Love 'em and Learn 'em
First, make friends, boost their morale
And fan their flickering hopes.
Tell 'em they can learn to read,
Of course they are not dopes!
Probe their psyche to feel out
How you best can reach 'em.
Then start testing what they know
And what you'll have to teach 'em.
When they start to read to you,
Listen in rapt awe,
Never notice when they trip,
Stumble, hem and haw.
Accompany each consonant,
Every faltering sound
With a due amount of praise
When success is found.
Clarify each point ahead,

Show no condescension,
Greet with ecstasy the first
Signs of comprehension.
Reassure the kid who flunks—That he's not a fool.
Tell him Thomas Edison—Never finished school.

—BABBIE LANGSDORF

MATERIALS SUGGESTED

Conquests in Reading, W. Kottmeyer and K. Ware, Webster Division, McGraw-Hill Book Company, Manchester, Mo. 63011. (Beginner–3rd grade)

Eye and Ear Fun, Grade levels 1–4, Clarence Stone et al., Webster Division, McGraw-Hill Book Company, Manchester, Mo. 63011.

A First Course in Phonic Reading, G. Helson, Educators Publishing Service, Inc., Cambridge, Mass. 02138. (Beginner)

Let's Read (linguistic approach—word families), Clarence L. Barnhart, Bronxville, N.Y. 10708. (Workbooks and Readers) (1st–3rd grade)

Merrill Linguistic Readers, Series with Phonics Approach, Charles E. Merrill Publishing Co., Columbus, Ohio 43216. (Beginner–6th grade)

Modern Curriculum Press Basic Phonics Program, Modern Curriculum Press, Cleveland, Ohio 44136. (Beginner–3rd grade)

Phonics Is Fun (a linguistic approach emphasizing auditory skills), Modern Curriculum Press, Cleveland, Ohio 44136. (Beginner–3rd grade)

Phonics We Use (emphasis on auditory discrimination), Lyons and Carnahan Educational Publishers, Chicago, Ill. 60616. (1st–6th grade)

Phonovisual Series, Phonovisual Products Inc., P.O. Box 5625, Washington, D.C. 20016.

Primary Phonics Series (brief pamphlet readers using consonants and short vowels, and workbooks), Educators Publishing Service, Cambridge, Mass. 02138.

A Second Course in Phonics, G. Helson, Educators Publishing Service, Inc., Cambridge, Mass. 02138. (Beginner–3rd grade)

Stern Structural Reading Series, Random House, Inc., New York, N.Y. 10022. (Beginner–1st grade)

The Sullivan Associates Readers Series (fourteen books stressing short vowel sounds), McGraw-Hill Book Company, New York, N.Y.

For the Older Student

New Streamlined English Series, F. Laubach et al., New Readers Press, Syracuse, N.Y. 13210.

Solving Language Difficulties, Amey Steere, Caroline Z. Peck, Linda Kahn, Educators Publishing Co., Cambridge, Mass. 02138.

6 READING COMPREHENSION

Reading would be simplified if an author's thoughts could automatically pop out of a book and jump into the reader's mind. If that were possible, it would only be necessary for a person to hold an open book in his hand and recognize printed words as his eyes travel across the page. Reading, however, is a complicated process and there is much more to reading than recognizing printed words. The reader has to understand what words mean in a particular sentence or paragraph, because words are merely symbols for ideas. A person who is reading must see ideas as well as words; otherwise he will turn pages and not have the faintest idea what he is reading. Reading with understanding requires thinking, and, of course, intelligence plays an influential role. As one might expect, a youngster's or adult's concentration, interest, motivation, and experiential background contribute to this understanding.

Language and thinking skills are the foundation of reading comprehension. An individual's understanding of what he reads will be determined to a large extent by the development of his language skills, knowledge of word connotations, sentence formation, and syntax. A child must understand a sentence before he can comprehend a paragraph. He must be taught that a paragraph is made up of sentences which are related to each other; it is a unit built around one main thought. The paragraph can stand alone or can be one of many related paragraphs that make up a chapter, article, or book.

In order to comprehend a paragraph, article or book, the reader must grasp the author's main thought, and discover what important facts and details the writer uses to support his thinking. What is more, the reader has to distinguish between important and unimportant details. Also, he often is required to infer meanings when an author does not express his thoughts, but only suggests them. Of equal importance is recognizing the author's plan in presenting his material. Many average or above-average students may experience aspects of comprehension problems similar to those of learning-disabled students.

A learning-disabled youngster may or may not have trouble with comprehension. On the one hand, Tony, a bright boy, had difficulty with word-attack skills. Once he overcame this problem, he read with excellent comprehension. On the other hand, Josie, equally bright and very verbal, quickly acquired basic reading skills, but she had great difficulty with the connotations of words. Consequently, her comprehension suffered and she did poorly in school. Being puzzled by the different connotations of words is only one of the problems affecting comprehension. It should be added that reading comprehension is a constellation of language, thinking and reading skills. Anyone with a weakness in one or more of these specific areas has difficulty understanding what he reads, no matter how intelligent he is. Of course, residual problems of word recognition will always impede comprehension.

To help a student read with better understanding, it is necessary to discover what particular weakness is contributing to his comprehension difficulties. Is it the understanding of words and/or sentence structure or the separation of the main thought from supporting details? Is it recognizing patterns of writing or drawing conclusions? Is it an emotional problem, lack of concentration, or something else?

The following techniques for comprehension are applicable to all ages and may be modified or expanded according to the student's needs. Since the emphasis in reading after the third and fourth grades is on vocabulary and comprehension, most of the techniques are geared to the upper elementary grades, junior and senior high school.

Techniques for Comprehension: Improving Language Skills

Understanding words

1. Teach new words and their meanings. Before reading a paragraph or short story, select words that might be unfamiliar. Discuss them. Have the child or older student use those words in spoken or written sentences.

   Use new words learned in the following exercises: Write a sentence with one of the new words deleted. Ask the learner to select from his list of new words the one that best completes the sentence. Example:

helpful.

The naughty dog is very (harmful)   harmful.
good.

See if the youngster can guess new words from the context. Examples of sentences and new words:

> *Johnny wanted a toy drum and he asked his mother how he could earn money to buy one. (2nd–3rd grade)*
>
> *It was not a time for anger; it was time to make amends. (6th–7th grade)*
>
> *If facts are presented too quickly, the mind cannot assimilate them and they are useless. (12th grade)*

Have the student keep a word file: Suggest he write each new word on one side of an index card. On the other side write its definition and a sentence using the word. Review the word periodically to be sure the student retains it. Put a check on the card every time he remembers it correctly. For this accomplishment, he can tear the card up or take it home after four or five checks.

2. Have the junior or senior high school student study word groups— words related to the same topic or general idea. Examples:

> *Books:* satire, romance, classic, tragedy, comedy, drama, etc.
>
> *Music:* solo, duet, lyrical.
>
> *Characteristics of people:* physical—vigorous, agile, homely; social—tactful, affable, arrogant, brusque.

Ask the student to use new words to describe a politician (moral and social characteristics) or a professional athlete (physical characteristics).

Have the student use new groups of words to write a want ad describing a criminal or a missing person.

Take the subject of ghosts, for example. Present the youngster with several new words related to that topic. Using a thesaurus, ask the student to find additional words that belong in that group: *ghosts*— apparitions, visions, phantoms (some additional words found— specters, illusions, spirits).

3. Have the student learn the special vocabulary he needs in the content fields. Each subject has its own particular vocabulary which varies according to grade levels. A student cannot understand what he reads in any subject unless he understands the words that are commonly used in that field. Examples:

> *Social studies and history:* agriculture, climate, manufacture,

territory, democratic, conservative, amendment, impeachment, abolitionist, despotism

Mathematics: equation, dividend, numerator, denominator, circumference, vertical, adjacent, equidistant, binomial, tangent

Science: erosion, combustion, bacteria, calorie, gravity, condensation, evaporation, insoluble, opaque, photosynthesis

Literature: plot, background, character, climax, anecdote, commentary, bibliography, exposition, monologue, paraphrase

Suggest that the student look up the definition of words in a specific subject that might be unfamiliar to him.

Make up a game of vocabulary lotto with specialized words. Put vocabulary words on a grid. Write their definitions on individual cards. To play the game, the student must match the definition to the correct word. He tries to match all the definitions to the words within a specified time limit.

Emancipate	Abolition	Compromise	Federal
Delegate	Judicial	Fugitive	Senate
Legislature	SOCIAL STUDIES WORDS		Arsenal
Secession	Repeal	Petition	Policy
Extradition	Annex	Negotiate	Commander

withdrawal of a state from the nation

(This is an excellent classroom or small group activity. Students can make up lotto games in different subjects, which they can exchange with each other.)

4. Work with students on different connotations of words (example: *bear* a burden; *bear*, the animal). See chapter 4.

5. Directly related to understanding words is knowing different parts of speech—nouns, verbs, adjectives, and adverbs—and their functions. Some students, particularly the learning-disabled, may be confused by the general shift in grammatical usage, which in turn hampers their reading comprehension. Help a youngster understand this: Show him that the same word can be used as a noun, verb, adjective. For example, *fire:*

    > as a noun—The *fire* started in a pile of leaves.
    > as a verb—He will *fire* his gun.
    > as an adjective—The *fire* extinguisher was above the door.

    Ask a youngster to make up his own sentences using the same word as a noun, verb, adjective. Some possible words: fly, labor, spring, telephone, profit, polish, charge, train, supply, storm, answer.

6. Point out that words can shift their forms when used as different parts of speech. For example: *enjoy* (verb), *enjoyment* (noun), *enjoyable* (adjective), *enjoyably* (adverb).

    On a piece of paper draw four columns. Give the student one form of a word and ask him to find the other three forms and put them in the proper column. Words given are underscored: answers are in parentheses.

Noun	Verb	Adjective	Adverb
success	(succeed)	(successful)	(successfully)
(nation)	nationalize	(national)	(nationally)
(preference)	(prefer)	preferable	(preferably)
(profit)	(profit)	(profitable)	profitably

Show the student that certain word endings are clues to parts of speech:

ENDINGS INDICATING WORDS
THAT NAME—NOUNS

-ness	(harshness)	-tion	(production)
-ment	(advertisement)	-ty	(cruelty)
-or	(contractor)	-ance	(appearance)
-ist	(tourist)	-er	(buyer)

ENDINGS INDICATING WORDS
THAT SHOW ACTION—VERBS

-ize	(harmonize)	-ify	(horrify)
-ate	(officiate)	-en	(sharpen)

ENDINGS INDICATING WORDS
THAT DESCRIBE—ADJECTIVES

-ive	(active)	-al	(musical)
-able	(believable)	-ous	(desirous)
-ible	(edible)	-ful	(restful)
-y	(shaky)	-less	(careless)

7. Explain to the youngster the meaning of a root word, that it is the basic part of a word before a beginning (prefix) or an ending (suffix) has been added. Other words can be derived from its root or base: happy, unhappy; thought, thoughtful.

Teach the youngster the meanings of the most important prefixes and suffixes. These can be found in many vocabulary books. Have the student supplement work in these books by making the following type of card:

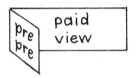

Use the words studied in sentences.

On the high school level, help the student learn the meaning of foreign roots, such as *ject* (throw); *mort, mors* (death). Vocabulary books will provide exercises in combining prefixes and suffixes with these roots to form different words.

8. One cannot understand the meaning of a word if he does not accent it correctly. Look at the same word accented differently: one makes sense; the other does not. For example, the at'ri cal, the at ri'cal.

Before you can give a student general rules about accent, be sure he can hear himself stressing different parts of words. Locating the accent is not easy for many learning-disabled children because they do not hear it readily. However, they will catch on with practice and drill. Practice finding the accented syllable. Then mark it with the symbol (') that indicates accent. For example, hos'pi tal, in struc'tive.

Teach a youngster generalizations about accent:

a. The accent usually falls on the root word, practically never on a prefix or suffix: fright'ful, re call'.

b. Most two- and three-syllable words are accented on the first syllable: gov'ern ment, cyl'in der, frus'trate, lim'it.

c. The addition of a suffix often causes a change in accent: tim'id, tim id'i ty; frag'ment, frag men tar'y.

9. Show how the meanings of words can change by shifting the accent. For example: con tent' (pleased, satisfied); con'tent (what is contained in something).

The following type of exercise can be helpful. Take a word—for example, convict (con vict). Ask the student to write the word in the blank space and mark the correct accent.

The jury may (<u>con vict'</u>) the man for burglary.
The (<u>con'vict</u>) was taken to prison by the guards.

10. Be alert to words that are often confused because they have a similar overall appearance—for example, *petition, partition*—or have slight differentiation in sound—*imminent, eminent.* When these words are confused, they hinder comprehension. These words are particularly perplexing to children with perceptual difficulties, auditory and visual problems.

Give a youngster a sentence with a misused word. Ask him to identify it and to substitute the correct word.

He excepted *the invitation to the party. (accepted)*
The teacher asked the children to be quite. *(quiet)*

Have the reader fill in the missing words in a sentence or paragraph from a choice of words. This is called the cloze technique, used in many workbooks and in many standardized reading tests. For example:

They floated down the (1) _____ *on a log raft. The water was calm so they had a (2)* _____ *trip.*
    (1) road <u>river</u> path
    (2) rough dangerous <u>quiet</u>

Older children would have fun reading *The Rivals* by Richard Sheridan, and selecting lines spoken by Mrs. Malaprop, who was famous for her misuse of English words. (Comical misuse of English words is now known as malapropisms.)

"This very day I have interceded *another letter from the fellow."* *(intercepted)*
"I would by no means wish a daughter of mine to be a progeny." *(prodigy)*

Students enjoy making up their own malapropisms and having their classmates detect them.

Understanding sentences, sentence structure, and syntax

1. Explain that a sentence is a group of words expressing a complete thought.

2. Show how a sentence can be expanded in order to add information and meaning.

The cowboy rode. (Start with a noun, cowboy, and a verb, rode.)

The strong cowboy rode. (Add a describing word, *strong.*)

The strong cowboy rode a horse. (Add an object, *horse.*)

Yesterday, the strong cowboy rode a horse on the prairie. (Add words designating time and place: *yesterday, prairie.*)

3. Write an expanded sentence and have the child point out the word or words that answer the following questions:

Who (is the sentence about)?

What (happened)?

When (did it happen)?

Where (did it happen)?

How (did it happen)?

During recess, Jane kicked the ball high over the fence

 when   who   what   how   where

4. Directly related to understanding sentences is knowing the role of different parts of speech. Teach the child the function of a noun, verb, adjective, adverb.

Grammar can be taught in many ways—the linguistic approach, the traditional approach, and often a combination of both. A child with specific language problems seems to respond best to traditional methods and a concrete approach, using familiar situations.

In the process of teaching grammar, have the child find nouns, verbs, and adjectives around him:

At Home	At School
nouns: porch, lamp, dish	blackboard, desk, ruler
verbs: washing, cooking	writing, drawing
adjectives: neat, warm	quiet, noisy

Take a picture. Ask the youngster to list the nouns, verbs, adjectives that he sees in the picture.

Act out different parts of speech with the student. Take one part of speech, *adjective*, for example. Ask the student to select an adjective, and act it out. You try to guess it.

Play *Mad Libs.*

A special problem in grammar which affects reading comprehension is the use of pronouns in their many forms. A common stumbling block is identifying pronouns and their antecedents. Much practice is needed in finding the reference for the pronoun.

Sally wanted a new dress and went shopping with her mother. She *found just the dress* she *wanted.*

(*She refers to* Sally)

Learning-disabled children are particularly confused by pronouns.

5. Show the youngster that the order of words in a sentence will affect its meaning:

> *The boy ate a hot dog.*
> *A hot dog ate the boy.*

Ask the youngster to rearrange a group of words to make a sentence that makes sense:

> *leaves girl raked the many*
> *morning they tomorrow tennis play will*

Ask students to make up scrambled sentences for their classmates.

In working with sentences, be sure to teach or review the concepts of *subject*—the part of the sentence which is talked about; and *predicate*—the part of the sentence which talks about the subject.

Help the student understand complex sentences. (Students find complex sentences confusing because they have difficulty selecting the main clause from the subordinate clause and often miss the main idea.)

Explain to the student that a complex sentence generally has one thought that is more important than another. For example: *After he left school, Tom went to football practice.* The important thought in this sentence is "Tom went to football practice." It can stand alone and is called the main, principal, or independent clause. "After he left school" is less important. It does not express a complete thought and cannot stand alone. It is called a dependent or a subordinate clause.

Point out that in the above sentence *after* is a clue word. Words like after, before, since, because, if, when, etc. are clues to subordinate clauses. Ask the student to use them in sentences.

Compound sentences—two simple sentences joined by a conjunction—do not present many problems. An example: *We remembered the potatoes and onions but we forgot the string beans.*

Understanding paragraphs

1. Finding the main thought: Preparatory to finding the main thought in reading, use pictures. Show a child or student a picture. Ask him what it is about—what name would he give the picture, like a title to a book.

Have a youngster read a paragraph at his grade level, followed by a question which may clue him in to the main idea:

AVERAGE 3RD GRADE

An owl's eyes are the most interesting thing about him. They are at the front of his head. Other birds' eyes are at the sides of their heads. An owl can't turn his eyes from side to side. He must turn

*his whole head when he wants to see something at the side. An owl
sees better at night than he does in the daytime.*[1]

What does this paragraph tell about an owl?
a. Things that make its eyes interesting
b. What makes the owl the wisest of all birds
c. How owls' eyes differ from people's eyes

AVERAGE 9TH GRADE

*According to biographies, General George Patton had a constitu-
tional weakness—a reading disability. "Old Blood and Guts," as
he was named, could not read at the age of twelve and never
learned to read well. Yet, he was a fluent speaker whether quoting
poetry or indulging in profanity. Moreover, his outstanding
memory was a redeeming ability. By memorizing lectures and
texts and recalling them word for word, he compensated for his
reading problems and he managed to graduate from West Point.*

What is the main idea of this paragraph?
a. General Patton had an extraordinary memory.
b. General Patton could not read when he was twelve.
c. General Patton had a reading disability.*
d. General Patton was an excellent speaker.

2. Finding the topic sentence: Explain that the topic sentence expresses
   the main thought of a paragraph. It is often found at the beginning of a
   paragraph, but may be found in the middle or at the end. Sometimes the
   topic sentence is implied. Other times it is repeated. Occasionally there
   is no topic sentence and the reader has to infer the writer's thoughts.

EXAMPLES

*A male sea lion makes a jealous husband. Like Eastern sultans, he
assembles a harem and closely guards his wives. If one is stolen by
another male, he pursues the stealthy suitor and battles furiously
for repossession.*

*A roaring fireplace is beautiful and dramatic but it is not an
efficient heater for large rooms in frigid weather. For comfort,
fireplace warmth must be supplemented by oil or gas heat. Due to
soaring fuel costs, the inset stove for fireplaces is becoming popular. In appearance this inset stove, which sits inside the firebox,
resembles the old-fashioned coal or wood burning stove. It hasn't*

---

[1]Reprinted by permission of the publisher from *Gates-Peardon Reading Exercises, Prepara
tory Level A* (New York: Teachers College Press, copyright © 1963 by Teachers College,
Columbia University. All rights reserved.), exercise 6.

the charm of glowing logs but it heats more effectively and lowers fuel bills.

Don't you think snakes are fortunate? They never require a face lift. Frequently, they shed their skins and develop new ones all on their own. These are lustrous and handsome. What is more, false dentures are never a necessity. When their teeth fall out, they grow new ones. Because snakes can renew their youth, they are symbols for life eternal in many Eastern religions.

3. Finding important details: Explain to the student that details are necessary to clarify the main idea and add information. Once he has found the main idea of a passage, he can look for details; moreover, he must learn to separate the important from the unimportant ones—those which are not essential.

   Ask the youngster to read a paragraph and select the main idea. Then ask him specific questions, which will clue him in to important details. (These questions can be applied to most types of writing.)

   Benjamin Franklin was a famous inventor who lived in Philadelphia from 1706 to 1790. Science was one of his main interests. He proved that lightning was a form of electricity. As a result of this discovery, he constructed the first lightning rod. Another of his scientific contributions was a stove that could be safely kept in the house and did not smoke.

   What happened?
   What is the story about?
   When did it take place?
   Whom is the story about?
   Where did it take place?
   Why did it happen?

   Other paragraphs may suggest other types of questions:

   What was the problem?
   How was it solved?

   Tell the student he should keep questions like these in his mind when he reads.

   Give the student a paragraph to read and ask him to separate the main idea from the details in the following manner:

   Penguins are strange birds that live in the Antarctic. They look like little men with their black coats and white fronts. Penguins walk upright on weblike feet. Although they swim and dive, they do not fly.

Main Idea	*Details*
Penguins are strange birds that live in the Antarctic.	They look like little men with their black coats and white fronts.
	Penguins walk upright on weblike feet.
	Although they swim and dive, they do not fly.

Have the student read a paragraph and separate the main idea from supporting details by placing boxes around them in the following manner:

> Penguins are strange birds that live in the Antarctic.

> They look like little men with their black coats and white fronts.

> Penguins walk upright on their weblike feet.

> Although they swim and dive, they do not fly.

Have the student underline the main idea and number the supporting details.

Nothing involves more accurate reading of details than following directions—whether taking a test, writing a paper, filling out forms, making a model, repairing a machine, or cooking a meal. Not only must the child or adult understand what he is supposed to do and how, but he must pay attention to command words, like *define, compare, summarize,* or *put your last name first.* In addition, directions must be followed in order. This is difficult for the learning-disabled student who has sequencing problems; he may need extra practice following directions. All of us, however, have run into trouble when we have read directions carelessly.

4. Teach the youngster to draw conclusions from questions. Ask questions that require interpretive answers:

Why do we wash our hands before eating?
Why do we have crossing guards?

PICTURES

Ask a young child questions which require drawing conclusions about illustrations in his primer or reader. About a picture of two children sledding in bright sunlight, ask a child "What time of day is it?" "What is the weather like?"

Ask a slightly older child questions about a picture, such as the one depicting purse-snatching on p. 34. "How did the girl feel?" "What were the witnesses thinking?"

Ask an older student to interpret a cartoon.

TELEVISION PROGRAMS

Discuss different types of programs with the youngster—detective stories, comedies, family situations. See if he can:

Tell you the story in the proper order of events

Describe the time and place

Describe the behavior of the characters

Tell you why something happened and what was the result

This is a particularly good medium for learning for the learning-disabled child; he enjoys watching television and is not threatened by it.

CHARADES

Act out the title of a book, play, or poem with a young child or a small group of children. Help them find clues and use them in guessing what that title is.

ACTING

Make up an imaginary scene, such as a burglary. Have the youngster be the detective who has to look for clues and solve the problem.

5. Interpreting what you read: Have a student practice making associations—seeing what several ideas have in common. Give him two words; ask him how they are related. (This is sometimes hard for the learning-disabled child.)

> London and Paris
> Neil Armstrong and John Glenn
> Babe Ruth and Lou Gehrig
> (Answers should have a few details: London and Paris are both large cities, capitals, in Western Europe.)

Help a reader relate his own experiences or background information to what he is about to read. Combining his old ideas with new ideas will add meaning to his reading. If a child is about to read *Hans Brinker and the Silver Skates*, ask him what he knows about Holland. Has he read another story about Holland, such as *The Boy and the Dike*? Has he seen pictures on television or in magazines about Holland? Show him pictures of Holland—of tulips, windmills, wooden shoes—from books and magazines such as the *National Geographic.*

If students are going to read *The Red Badge of Courage,* discuss the Civil War. Some students may have been to Gettysburg, Bull Run, or Vicksburg. Have them share experiences. Discuss the lyrics of Civil War songs such as "The Battle Hymn of the Republic" and "Marching Through Georgia." Discuss other books about war and the feelings of soldiers in battle which the students may have read, such as *All Quiet on the Western Front.* Supplement information from more books and periodicals for the learning-disabled youngster who may have limited knowledge and meager reading experience.

Teach the student to make inferences in reading—to draw conclusions from stated facts. Tell him facts are often hints about the character, setting, and mood of a story. Ask him questions which help him make inferences. The following paragraphs are for average 9th–10th graders.

"THE FRILL"

"My dear, the only way to manage these native tailors is to be firm!"

Mrs. Lowe, the postmaster's wife, settled herself with some difficulty into the wicker rocking-chair upon the wide veranda of her house. She was a large woman, red-faced from more food than necessary and little exercise over the ten-odd years she had spent in a port town on the China coast. Now as she looked at her caller and thus spoke, her square hard-fleshed face grew a little redder. Beside her stood a Chinese manservant who had just announced in a mild voice: "Tailor have come, missy."[2]

SAMPLE LEADING QUESTIONS

1. What do the facts about Mrs. Lowe's appearance and conversation suggest about her character?
2. What do the facts tell about Mrs. Lowe's lifestyle?
3. What do the facts tell about class distinctions in China?

"THE OUTCASTS OF POKER FLAT"

As Mr. John Oakhurst, gambler, stepped into the main street of Poker Flat on the morning of the twenty-third of November, 1850, he was conscious of a change in its moral atmosphere since the preceding night. Two or three men, conversing earnestly together, ceased as he approached, and exchanged significant glances. There was a Sabbath

[2]Pearl S. Buck, "The Frill," in *Short Stories,* ed. H.C. Schweikert (New York: Harcourt Brace Jovanovich, Inc., 1947), p. 322.

lull in the air, which, in a settlement unused to Sabbath influences, looked ominous.[3]

SAMPLE LEADING QUESTIONS

1. What do the facts suggest about the setting? What type of place is Poker Flat? Where do you think it is located?
2. What do the facts tell about the plight of John Oakhurst?
3. What makes the mood tense?

Have the student make mental pictures as he reads. These will add meaning to the story, poem, or play and help him remember what he is reading. In the following paragraph from "The Open Hearth" by H.S. Hall it is easy to visualize the bleakness of the steel mill town on an early November morning and sense the dreariness and grimness of the workers. This paragraph is for average 8th–9th graders.

It was a very black and a very dirty street down which I made my way that November morning at half-past five. There was no sidewalk; there were no lights. Rain had been falling for several days, and I waded through seas of mud and sloshed through lakes of water. There were men in front of me and men behind me, all plodding along through the muck and mire, just as I was plodding along, their tin lunch pails rattling as mine was rattling. Some of us were going to work, some of us were going to look for work—the steel mills lay somewhere in the darkness ahead of us.[4]

Sometimes facts are not given and the reader must gain insight by sensing the author's meaning. Often poetry is a good example of this type of expression. Have the student think about what the poet is trying to express in the following poem:

1. How does she use her imagination?
2. What feelings, beliefs is the poet trying to express?

I never saw a Moor—
I never saw the Sea—
Yet know I how the Heather looks
And what a Billow be.

I never spoke with God
Nor visited in Heaven—

---

[3]Bret Harte, "The Outcasts of Poker Flat," in *Great Short Stories*, ed. William Schramm (New York: Harcourt Brace Jovanovich, Inc., 1950), p. 94.

[4]Herschel S. Hall, "The Open Hearth."

Yet certain am I of the spot
As if the Checks were given—

——EMILY DICKINSON[5]

Among the many skills necessary for reading with understanding is *reading in thought units*. Recognizing groups of words that belong together enhances comprehension just as it can be impeded by incorrectly grouping words and reading word by word. When we speak, we naturally express ourselves in thought groups and not in isolated words: *Johnny shouted,/ "Watch out!/ You'll hit the ball/through the window."* We know exactly what Johnny yelled because his pattern of words was meaningful. Because of his wondrous built-in aptitude for language, a child learns to speak in thought units at an early age.

A youngster's or adult's comprehension would be hampered and slowed down if he read this sentence pausing between each word or grouping words improperly: *Johnny/shouted, "Watch/out! You'll/hit the/ ball through/the window."* A learning-disabled youngster with difficulty ordering words or seeing thought units will need special help in this area.

Students should be encouraged to read sentences in meaningful parts, such as prepositional phrases (inside the house, by the stream), clauses (when it rains, because we are sad), and descriptive phrases (the long winding country lane). Reading in thought units is usually taught in conjunction with rate of reading. (See Chapter 10.) Word by word reading must be discouraged as soon as possible. Thought units are often emphasized by punctuation. Punctuation signals how the writer wants a person to read a sentence—when to pause (, . ; : —), when to question (?), when to emphasize (!). In other words, attending to punctuation aids comprehension.

What makes a good reader? For some, natural endowment is a prime factor. It is often combined with a strong attraction to the printed page, which starts at an early age. For the reading majority, however, it is environment and a good teacher.

A good teacher combines her competence in teaching skills with warmth and encouragement. Furthermore, her own love of reading can stimulate and spark her students, even if they are learning disabled.

Penny was a learning-disabled child, who liked to listen to stories and poems, but hated to read. This was not surprising since the decoding of words had been an obstacle course for her since the first grade. Frustrated and discouraged, she shunned books whenever she could and would not even open any of the attractive, colorful ones her parents brought home

---

[5]Reprinted by permission of the publishers and the Trustees of Amherst College from THE POEMS OF EMILY DICKINSON, edited by Thomas H. Johnson, Cambridge: The Belknap Press of Harvard University Press, Copyright 1951. © 1955, 1979 by the President and Fellows of Harvard College.

from the library. Although she had a high I.Q., she was reading at third grade level in fifth grade. She was then diagnosed as being dyslexic.

Working with persistence and effort, Penny responded to tutoring. Although she did not object to workbook drills, she would not read a storybook with her tutor. However, she begged to hear stories if they were read to her and enjoyed discussing the characters and the plots. Highly intelligent, Penny had mature insight and curiosity. Her tutor sensed that she would become an ardent reader once her attitude toward reading changed.

Aware that reversing attitudes takes time, the tutor proceeded slowly and did not even suggest to the child that she could borrow a book. Moreover, she counseled Penny's intellectual parents to soft-pedal their own attitude toward her reading habits and to be patient.

One day Penny delightedly reported that she had been chosen to be the princess in the school performance of the Sleeping Beauty. When the tutor remarked that it might be fun to read some plays together, Penny acquiesced. It was not long before she became an enthusiastic play-reader who read her lines with feeling and good expression. The plays selected were all at her third grade reading level.

Several weeks later the tutor opened a storybook instead of a play. She had chosen a perennial favorite, *The Box Car Children* by Gertrude Chandler Warner, and said "Let's read this book together; I think you will like it." Penny did and, at the close of the lesson, asked if she could take the book home. She was finally on her way! She read *The Box Car Children* over and over again and soon was on to reading other stories and poetry. This successful reading experience transformed Penny from a frustrated little girl who hated reading into a child who suddenly was excited by the world of books.

MATERIALS SUGGESTED

Vocabulary

1101 Words You Need to Know, Murray Bromberg and Melvin Gordon, Barron's Educational Series, Inc., Woodbury, N.Y.

Thirty Days to a More Powerful Vocabulary, W. Funk and N. Lewis, Washington Square Press, New York, N.Y. 10003.

Vocabulary Builder Series, Books VII–I (grades 7–12), Austin M. Works, Educators Publishing Service, Inc., Cambridge, Mass. 02138.

Vocabulary for the College Bound, Harold Levine, AMSCO School Publications, Inc., New York, N.Y. 10013.

Vocabulary for the High School Student, Harold Levine, AMSCO School Publications, Inc., New York, N.Y. 10013.

Vocabulary through Pleasurable Reading, Harold Levine, AMSCO School Publications, Inc., New York, N.Y. 10013.

Word Games, Alice Farhas, Word Games, Healdsburgh, Ca. 95448.

Word Game Series, six books, all reading levels, Word Games, P.O. Box 305, Department 8, Healdsburgh, Ca. 95448.

Word Wealth, W. Miller, Holt, Rinehart & Winston, New York, N.Y. 10017.

Wordly Wise 1–7 (grades 4–10), Educators Publishing Service, Inc., Cambridge, Mass. 02138.

Understanding Sentences: Grammar and Syntax

Basic Grammar Skills, grades 4–8, Doris Kitchens and Margaret Zeff, Creative Teaching Press, Inc., Huntington Beach, Ca. 92649.

Exercises in English Grammar, Books 1 and 2, John H. Traenor, Educators Publishing Service, Inc., Cambridge, Mass. 02138.

Keys to Good Language, originated by Elizabeth Price Culp, The Economy Press, Oklahoma City, Okla.

Language Push-ups, Performance Level C, Diane K. McCarty, Harper and Row, Publishers, Inc., New York, N.Y.

Learning Grammar through Writing, Sandra Bell and James Wheeler, Educators Publishing Service, Inc., Cambridge, Mass. 02138.

Understanding English, Maryjane Carrell, Frank E. Richards Publishing Co., Inc., Phoenix, N.Y. 13135.

Workbooks for Elementary and Junior High Students

Basic Reading Skills for Junior High, Scott, Foresman & Company, Glenview, Ill. 60025. (Grade 7)

Be a Better Reader, Basic Skills Edition, Levels A–E, Nila Banton Smith, Prentice-Hall, Inc., Englewood Cliffs, N.J. 07632. (Grades 4–8)

Gates-Peardon Practice Exercises in Reading, Teachers College Press, New York, N.Y. 10017. (Grades 1–7)

Kaleidoscope, Wyatt et al., Field Education Publishers, Inc., San Francisco, Ca. 94105. (Grades 4–8)

New Practice Readers, Books A–G, Clarence R. Stone, Webster Division, McGraw-Hill Book Company, Manchester, Mo. 63011. (Grades 2–7)

Practicing Reading, Anne Marie Meuser, Random House, Inc., New York, N.Y. 10022. (Grades 1–8)

Reader's Digest Reading Skill Builders, Educational Division, Reader's Digest Services, Inc., Pleasantville, N.Y. 10570. (Grades 2–6)

Reading for Concepts, Books A–H, William Liddle, Webster Division, McGraw-Hill Book Company, Manchester, Mo. 63011. (Grades 3–9)

Reading for Meaning Series, J.B. Lippincott Company, Philadelphia, Pa. 19105. (Grades 4–8)

Reading and Thinking Skills, The Continental Press, Inc., Elizabethtown, Pa. 17022. (Grades 1–6)

Special Primary Series, L. Schwartz, Noble & Noble, New York, N.Y. 10017. (For urban disadvantaged children—interest level for elementary school grades) (Primer)

Specific Skill Builders, eight booklets: Using the Context, Following Directions, Detecting the Sequence, etc., Richard Boning, Barnell-Loft, Inc., Baldwin, N.Y. 11510. (Grades 2–9)

Tactics in Reading, Basic Reading Skills Series, Books I and II, Scott, Foresman & Company, Glenview, Ill. 60025. (Grades 7–8)

Basal Reading Programs: Basal Reading Series used in schools have accompanying workbooks.

High Interest/Low Vocabulary Books for Children with Reading Difficulties

Chandler Reading Books, Chandler Publishing Co., San Francisco, Ca. 94105. (Primer–6)

Cowboy Sam Series, Dan Frontier Series, Sailor Jack Series, Benefic Press, Roosevelt Rd., Westchester, Ill. 60153. (Primer–4)

Deep Sea Adventure Series, Field Educational Publications, San Francisco, Ca. 94105. (Interest—child to adult) (Grades 1–5)

Jim Forest Series, Harr Wagner Publishing, Field Educational Publications, San Francisco, Ca. 94105. (Grades 1–3)

Morgan Bay Mystery Series, Field Educational Publications, San Francisco, Ca. 94105. (Grades 2–4)

Books to Encourage Readers 3rd–6th Grade Level

B is for Betsy Series, Eddie's Pay Dirt, Carolyn Haywood, William Morrow & Co., Inc., New York, N.Y. 10016.

The Box Car Children Series, Gertrude Chandler Warner, Scott, Foresman & Company, Glenview, Ill. 60025.

Danny Dunn Series, Jay Williams, McGraw-Hill Book Company, New York, N.Y.

Encyclopedia Brown Series, Donald Sobel, Thomas Nelson and Sons, Nashville, Tenn. 32203.

Henry Huggins (and others), Beverly Cleary, William Morrow & Co., Inc., New York, N.Y. 10016.

The Little House on the Prairie Series, Laura Ingals Wilder, Harper & Row, Publishers, Inc., New York, N.Y.

Matthew Looney, Jerome Beatty, Young Scott Books, Addison-Wesley Publishing Co., Inc., Reading, Mass. 01867.

McGurk Mysteries, E.W. Hildeck, Macmillan, Inc., New York, N.Y. 10022.

Mystery Series, Gertrude Chandler Warner, Scott, Foresman & Company, Glenview, Ill. 60025.

Then Again, Maybe I Won't, Are You There God? It's Me, Margaret, Blubber, and others, Judy Blume, The Bradbury Press, Inc., Scarsdale, N.Y. 10583.

Magazines for Elementary School Children

Animals, Massachusetts Society for the Prevention of Cruelty to Animals, Boston, Mass.

Highlights, Highlights for Children, Inc., 2300 W. Fifth Avenue, Columbus, Ohio 43216.

National Geographic World, National Geographic Society, 17th and M Streets, N.W., Washington, D.C. 20036.

Ranger Rick, National Wildlife Federation, Vienna, Va.

Workbooks for Older Students

Be a Better Reader, Basic Skills Edition Levels, F–I, Nila Banton Smith, Prentice-Hall, Inc., Englewood Cliffs, N.J. 07632. (Grades 9–12)

Breaking the Reading Barrier, D.W. Gilbert, Prentice-Hall, Inc., Englewood Cliffs, N.J. 07632. (H.S.–College)

College Reading Skills, K. Blake, Prentice-Hall, Inc., Englewood Cliffs, N.J. 07632. (College)

Comprehension Skill Series, G. Williston, Jamestown Publishers, Providence, R.I. (J.H.S.–College)

Design for Good Reading, A–D, Schumacher et al., Harcourt Brace Jovanovich, Inc., New York, N.Y. 10017. (Grades 9–12)

Efficient Reading, J. Brown, D.C. Heath & Co., Lexington, Mass. 02173. (H.S.–College)

Increasing Reading Efficiency, L. Miller, Holt, Rinehart & Winston, Inc., New York, N.Y. 10017. (H.S.–College)

Modern College Reading, D. Milan, Charles Scribner's Sons, New York, N.Y. 10017. (H.S.–College)

Quest: Academic Skills Program. Harcourt Brace Jovanovich, Inc., New York N.Y. 10017. (H.S.–College)

Reader's Digest Advanced Reading Skill Builders, Reader's Digest Services, Inc., Pleasantville, N.Y. 10570. (Grades 7–8)

Reading Drills for Speed and Comprehension, Jamestown Publishers, Providence, R.I. (Grade 11–College)

Reading for Meaning Series, J.B. Lippincott Company, Philadalphia, Pa. 19105. (Grades 9–12)

Reading Success Series, Score 1–6, for 10- to 16-year-olds, Xerox Educational Publications, Columbus, Ohio 43216. (Workbooks for remedial training with a mature format. Basic skills are introduced sequentially from Book One through Book Six.)

Scope/Reading Skills (high interest level for teenagers and adults), Scholastic Book Services, New York, N.Y. 10036. (Grades 4–5)

Selections from the Black, 3 levels, E. Spargo, Jamestown Publishers, Providence, R.I. (Grade 7–College)

Tactics in Reading: Basic Reading Skills, Scott, Foresman & Company, Glenview, Ill. 60025. (Grades 9–12)

Topics for the Restless, E. Spargo, Jamestown Publishers, Providence, R.I. (Grade 7–College)

The Turning Point in Reading, D.W. Gilbert, Prentice-Hall, Inc., Englewood Cliffs, N.J. 07632. (Grades 9–10)

Why, What, How to Read, Lo Slater, Random House, Inc., New York, N.Y. 10022. (H.S.–College)

Magazines for Older Students

National Geographic Magazine, National Geographic Society, 17th and M Streets, N.W., Washington, D.C. 20036.

News for You, New Readers Press, Laubach Literacy, 112½ E. Fayette St., Box 131, Syracuse, N.Y. (High interest for adolescents and adults)

Know Your World, Xerox Education Publications, Education Center, Columbus, Ohio 43216. (For slow readers at two levels of difficulty)

Scope, Scholastic Magazines, Inc., New York, N.Y.

Dictionaries

Exploring Language with the Dictionary, Levels A–D (grades 3–6), Donna Rosenbauer, Prentice-Hall, Inc., Englewood Cliffs, N.J. 07632.

Macmillan Dictionary for Children, Macmillan, Inc., New York, N.Y. 10011.

Thorndike-Barnhart Dictionaries (beginning, intermediate, junior, advanced), Scott, Foresman & Company, Glenview, Ill. 60025.

Words to Know, a picture dictionary, H. Bricker and Y. Beckwith. Standard Educational Corporation, Chicago, Ill.

7 MATHEMATICS

While learning to understand the language of math may be a slippery path for the average child, it frequently can be a minefield to the learning-disabled child, who may stumble over not only difficult terms but ordinary words in unexpected usage.

Peter's mother said to him, "Now don't nag your father for a new bike. He's not working and these are difficult *times*. Do you know what I mean?" "Sure," answered Peter, "the nine *times* table is hard for me. But what has that to do with a new bike?"

In this chapter we are not speaking of students with an extreme inability to do arithmetic. Here we are concerned with children who do very poorly in math; they follow the normal developmental sequence in acquiring number concepts and skills but at a much slower rate. Generally, they lag two to three years behind. Furthermore, they are characterized by clinging to immature modes of thought and simplistic arithmetic methods instead of moving spontaneously to more advanced and efficient techniques. They do learn basic math skills, given time and competent assistance.

STAGES IN MATH

Expectations in math vary in different schools and different classrooms. The following are just *approximations* of many of the arithmetic skills a child is expected to learn.

IN THE PRESCHOOL YEARS
AND KINDERGARTEN

The following readiness skills introduce in direct and easy ways concepts of numbers and of numerals, which are symbols of numbers:

Knows meaning of words dealing with numbers, such as big, bigger, biggest; before, after; more, less, etc.

Places in order 6 blocks or cylinders, circles or squares, based on increasing size.

Counts orally to 30.

Counts to 10 pointing to each of 10 objects as he touch counts.

Identifies penny, nickel, dime.

Identifies a number group; 2 objects, 5 objects.

Matches equivalent sets (groups) 0–5.

Reads and writes numerals 0–10.

Matches numeral with set 0–5.

Finds the missing numerals of a series 0–10.

Finds one-half of a circle or a set of four items.

BY THE END OF FIRST GRADE

Identifies 0–50.

Counts orally 0–100.

Touch counts to 20.

Recognizes sets 6–10 and ordinals 1st–10th.

Matches numeral with set 6–10.

Reads and writes numerals 0–50.

Knows place value 0–50.

Renames 1's and 10's through 50—for example, 16 is the same as one 10 and 6 ones.

In addition: knows terms *add, sum, answer,* and *total;* knows facts 1–10; adds both horizontally and vertically; adds 2 digits—no regrouping, also called carrying.

In subtraction: knows terms *subtract, difference,* and *take away;* knows facts 1–10; subtracts both horizontally and vertically; subtracts 2 digits—no regrouping, also called borrowing.

Finds one-fourth of a shape or set.

Counts and writes by 10's to 100, by 5's to 50.

Knows penny = 1 cent, nickel = 5 cents, dime = 10 cents.

BY THE END OF SECOND GRADE

Reads and writes numerals 0–100. Matches numeral with number word 0–100.

Knows place value 50–100. (Place value is the value of a number because of the column it is in—ones, tens, hundreds, etc.)

Renames 50–100.

In addition, knows facts 11–20; adds 3 digits—no regrouping:

$$213$$
$$+\ \underline{142}$$

In subtraction, knows facts 11–20; subtracts 3 digits—no regrouping:

$$385$$
$$-\ \underline{162}$$

Solves one-step story problems.

Counts and writes by: 2's to 100, 3's to 36, 4's to 48, and 5's to 100.

Substitutes money values: penny, nickel, dime, quarter. For example, 1 dime = 10 pennies or 2 nickels.

BY THE END OF THIRD GRADE

Writes in sequence from memory 1–999.

Writes from dictation 1–999.

Renames 10's to 100's.

Knows Roman numerals I–X.

In addition: adds 2 and 3 digits with regrouping:

$$27 \qquad 274$$
$$+\ \underline{35} \quad +\ \underline{358}$$

In subtraction: subtracts 2 and 3 digits with regrouping:

$$46 \qquad 472$$
$$-\ \underline{19} \quad -\ \underline{185}$$

Checks result by addition.

In multiplication: learns tables, knows terms *product* and *times;* multiplies 2 and 3 digits by 1 digit:

$$42 \qquad 331$$
$$\times\ \underline{2} \quad \times\ \underline{3}$$

Multiplies multiples of 10's:

$$40$$
$$\times\ \underline{8}$$

In division: learns facts, knows terms *divisor* and *quotient;* divides with one-place divisor—$3\overline{)96}$; divides with remainder—$3\overline{)28}$; divides using multiples of 10—$30\overline{)600}$.

Solves two-step word problems using addition, subtraction, multiplication, and division.

Divides shapes and sets in ½, ¼, ⅓.

BY THE END OF FOURTH GRADE

Knows place value to millions.

Knows Roman numerals XI–C.

In addition: adds 1–3 digits with regrouping:

$$874$$
$$+\ 376$$

In subtraction: subtracts 2–4 digits with regrouping:

$$4238$$
$$-\ 3949$$

In multiplication: multiplies with regrouping:

$$58 \qquad 727$$
$$\times\ 3 \quad \times\ 6$$

Multiplies by 2 digits:

$$25$$
$$\times\ 12$$

Multiplies multiples of 100, 1000:

$$400 \qquad 6000$$
$$\times\ \ 3 \quad \times\ \ 20$$

In division, performs harder problems:

$$3\overline{)638} \quad 10\overline{)181}$$

Counts and writes by 6's to 72, 7's to 84, 8's to 96, and 9's to 108.

Solves multiple-step story problems using addition, subtraction, division, multiplication.

In fractions: knows terms *numerator* and *denominator;* adds and subtracts fractions with like denominators:

$$^2/_5 + {}^1/_5 =$$
$$^5/_6 - {}^2/_6 =$$

In measurement: finds perimeters—understands dry measurement.

BY THE END OF FIFTH GRADE

Reads and writes billions.

Knows Roman numerals C–M.

Understands rounding off whole numbers (25.7 becomes 26).

In addition: does problems with 4 and 5 columns:

$$2731 \qquad 7648 \qquad 25483$$
$$1285 \qquad 9026 \quad +\ 37642$$
$$+\ 2315 \qquad 2483$$
$$+\ 2315$$

In subtraction: subtracts 4 and 5 digits with regrouping:

$$14012$$
$$-\ \underline{5778}$$

In multiplication: multiplies 3 digits by 3 digits, 4 by 4:

$$
\begin{array}{cc}
587 & 6423 \\
\times\ \underline{362} & \times\ \underline{4052}
\end{array}
$$

In division: divides 2-digit divisor with remainder:

$$
\begin{array}{r}
53\ \text{r}\ 9 \\
45\overline{)2394}
\end{array}
$$

divides by 3-digit divisor:

$$240\overline{)5382}$$

In fractions: multiplication and division of fractions; finds equivalent fractions: $^4/_8 = {}^2/_4 = \frac{1}{2}$; adds unlike fractions: $^3/_5 + {}^5/_8$.

In decimals: identifies place value (tenths, hundredths, thousandths, etc.); adds, subtracts, and multiplies decimals; solves decimal fractions and equivalence.

Solves multiple-step problems using fractions and decimals.

In measurement: finds areas of squares and rectangles; uses solid measurement. In the early grades children learn what pint, quart, inch, foot, and yard are. They also learn that there is a metric system. Around third grade they begin to convert inches, feet, and yards, and around fourth grade, to work with the metric system. From fifth to sixth grade on, depending on the school, students use both systems in math and science.

FROM SIXTH GRADE UP

It is difficult to generalize about the level at which arithmetic skills are taught. For instance, some schools will delay teaching decimals until sixth grade. Naturally students are not able to do percentage problems until they can add, subtract, multiply, and divide decimals. Once it is possible for them to work with decimals, they can tackle practical arithmetic problems essential for everyday living, such as computation of interest, profit, loss, sales tax, discount, commissions, etc.

During the elementary school years, children are often grouped within the classroom according to their math performance. Once they reach middle school and junior high, they are often assigned to separate math classes—modified, regular, accelerated.

In high school there are special areas of math, such as algebra and geometry. As a rule, students with learning disabilities in math find these subjects extremely difficult, especially if they have spatial problems and have trouble remembering the number facts. Good math students will go on to trigonometry, pre-calculus, and sometimes calculus.

BASIC COMPETENCY

Some states have competency tests in math as a prerequisite for a high school diploma. Just what are the arithmetic skills necessary for competency? What are those arithmetic skills essential for survival in a world of discounts and of installment buying?

In general usage, basic competency in arithmetic means the ability to carry out paper and pencil computations in addition, subtraction, multiplication, and division with whole numbers, fractions, decimals, and percentages. It also includes measurement of geometric figures and computation of time, distance, weight, and volume. However, computational skills in isolation are insufficient; one must know when to multiply or divide in a given situation to achieve a desired goal, and how to check the correctness of the outcome. Computational skills, then, must be accompanied by the ability to select the appropriate operations and to judge the reasonableness of the results. For instance, in ordering ten items at $1.25, one should be able to recognize quickly that they would cost $12.50, not $125.

Additionally, a person cannot function easily in daily activities without having developed a certain degree of skill in mental arithmetic. When dealing with numbers, one must be able to make rough estimates. In a supermarket, when a shopper is worrying if there will be enough money to pay for a chicken, string beans, rice, bananas, and milk, he must estimate how much everything will cost. Frequently, we must mentally gauge time and distance as well as money. Competency also includes the ability to read maps and interpret tables, charts, and graphs.

LEARNING-DISABLED MATH STUDENTS

In our experience, learning-disabled math students fall roughly into two groups, those with language disorders and those having visual-spatial problems. However, it must be noted that it is rare that a student shows most characteristics of one group and none of the other.

Children with Language Disorders

Children who have marked difficulties with the language and symbols of reading frequently display similar difficulties with the language and symbols of arithmetic. What is more, the same lags in basic skills that affect reading affect math, such as:

POOR AUDITORY RECALL

1. Cannot remember the names of the numbers.

118

2. Slow to master the number facts, and in particular, may fail to memorize the multiplication tables—often recorded on school records in the middle grades.

3. Has difficulty holding numbers in his mind. For instance, in a column of addition, he cannot hold the sum of the first two numbers, 3 and 5, long enough to add the third, 7:

$$\left.\begin{array}{c} 3 \\ 5 \end{array}\right]$$ think 8

$$\underline{7}$$ plus $$\underline{7}$$

POOR SEQUENCING

1. Has trouble counting forward and backward, skip counting.

2. Cannot follow a multi-step procedure. For example, in a lengthy multiplication problem, a student might omit a step or take a step out of order. Sometimes an unnecessary step might be added which belongs to another procedure.

DIFFICULTY READING AND WRITING NUMBERS

Has difficulty with numbers whose names are not written the way they are spoken:

18 means eight-teen; he writes (or says) *81*

41 means forty-one; he writes (or says) *401*

201 means two hundred and one; he writes (or says) *2001*

LEFT-RIGHT ORIENTATION

1. Reverses writing numbers: 3 for 5.

2. Reverses reading numbers: 12 for 21; 274 for 472. In this example, the value of the numbers was changed by putting numerals in the wrong position, thereby giving them the wrong place value. The 2 should be in the ones column; the 7 in the tens column; the 4 in the hundreds column.

Place Value

100's	10's	1's
4	7	2

LANGUAGE

1. Displays weakness in mastering the vocabulary of number, spatial position, and spatial relationships, such as: more than, less than; greater, lesser; before, after; carry, borrow; numerator, denominator; prime numbers, prime facts.

2. These terms often cause confusion that persists long after the computational aspects of arithmetic are learned.

3. Word problems by their nature cause consternation to many school children and are a particular hurdle to the learning-disabled.

Children with Visual-Spatial Problems

This group, smaller in total number than the first group, shows visual-spatial weaknesses related to the ability to perceive and analyze spatial patterns in math. They are basically perceptual difficulties.

SPATIAL DISCRIMINATION

Poor spatial judgments when working with concrete materials, such as Cuisenaire rods, Stern rods, Uni-fix, or blocks of different sizes.

VISUAL PERCEPTION

1. Slow learning of relative position: for instance, on a number line, a child may be unable to tell if 3 is closer to 4 or to 7.

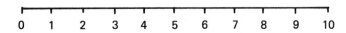

2. Cannot see similarities and differences in given figures. For example, a visual dot display may be processed incorrectly; the child may equate

$$x \, x \text{ with } x \, x \, x$$
$$x \, x \qquad x \, x \, x$$
$$\qquad x \, x \, x$$

$$x \quad \text{with } x$$
$$x \, x \qquad x \, x$$
$$\qquad x \, x \, x$$

☐ with ☐

when the task is to compare the number of units.

DISALIGNMENT

Difficulty in lining up numbers so that they are in the proper column. This leads to incorrect solutions–for example:

$$\begin{array}{r} 4 \ 3 \\ + \ 6 \\ \hline 109 \end{array}$$

POOR VISUAL-SPATIAL MEMORY

Inability to transfer between horizontal and vertical forms. For example:

$$3 + 6 = 9 \qquad \begin{array}{r} 3 \\ + \ 6 \\ \hline 9 \end{array}$$

(This problem may not be evident when a student is completing preprinted materials, but will appear when he copies sums, for example, or writes to dictation.) One learning-disabled student combined the above into one unique form:

3

+

6

=

9

VISUAL ROTATION

1. Confusion of signs due to visual rotation, such as + and ×, even when he understands the operation.
2. In the higher grades the forms and angulations in geometry and locating coordinates in algebra may be trouble spots.

Many of the children with visual-spatial problems have excellent math concepts. They figure all sorts of mental problems in their heads and surprise their elders by being whizzes at making change. They also perplex their parents by bringing home failing grades in math. Because of difficulty aligning numbers and other spatial problems, they have tremendous trouble doing arithmetic computation correctly. Some parents are amazed when after individual testing, they are told that their child is superior in math. Once these children overcome their spatial problems, they can do very well in math.

THE CASE OF RUTHIE

As we pointed out in Chapter 4, a child's thinking process evolves from perceptions gained first through sensory-motor experiences. (Remember the baby who touched the hot stove.) Therefore, it is not surprising that children with exceedingly immature visual-spatial perceptions are slower in concept development even though they may have average or above-average intelligence.

Seven-year-old Ruthie was a little girl with average intelligence and adequate language skills. Yet, perceptually she was like a five-year-old. She would try to squeeze herself under a low sofa because she could not perceive the difference in size (hers) and space (the space under the sofa). If she could not perceive size, how could she develop the concept? Moreover, she did not know her right side from her left, was confused about directionality and appeared extremely disorganized.

She was not ready to learn basic skills, especially math, which requires an understanding of size and space, directionality and order. Going back to sensory learning was necessary before Ruthie could tackle many of the basic skills. Consequently, she was sent to a physiotherapist who helped to make her aware of her body in space and spatial relationships. The therapist worked with Ruthie on laterality (right and left) and body movements, and worked closely with her mother, recommending follow-up exercises to do with Ruthie at home. In addition, she advised her to encourage the use of Ruthie's dominant hand. Ruthie showed mixed dominance and switched from the left to the right hand, but she indicated preference for the left. When she wrote with her left hand, her tendency to reverse letters and numbers was less apparent.

All of these procedures helped Ruthie improve her visual-spatial skills, paving the way for learning math. However, Ruthie's readiness for math was hindered by another problem. She could not sequence. So how could she count except by rote memory? She could not count in a meaningful way. For example, when we placed four lollipops in front of Ruth and asked her to count them by pointing, she pointed to one lollipop twice and left out two others. She was unable to count each item once and only once in order. This is referred to as one-to-one correspondence, an ability fundamental to the understanding of math.

Clearly, Ruthie was functioning on a five-year-old level. She judged everything by appearances and was bound by the nearest stimuli. Like the five-year-olds in Chapter 4, she thought that a neat pile of M and M's was much less than a pile scattered all over the table, even though the amount was the same in both. She had a long way to go before she could understand the basic concept of number, that is that the number of objects in a group stays the same no matter how they are arranged, which Piaget refers to as conservation of number.

Even when Ruthie was way behind, she showed the ability to learn when she was tutored individually in a structured situation where distractions were minimized. She first learned through the use of concrete material but eventually was able to transfer her math activities to paper and pencil tasks.

TECHNIQUES FOR MATH

Learning through Use of Concrete Materials and Motor Activities

Learning to count

- Readiness for one-to-one correspondence: Use activities that require matching. For example, in nursery school, at snack time: First, ask a child to move one chair to the table for herself. Then later ask her to move one for each child in her group. When the child is simultaneously doing and saying, as in counting aloud with each chair she moves to the table, she is providing her own practice and drill.
- Count on fingers; count real objects.

- Use counting games involving motor acts, such as pointing to three bears—one, two, three; taking six steps; counting out four cookies.

Learning sets, groups, and the conservation of number

- Match equivalent sets:

  four dolls, four dresses

  five children, five cookies

- Have the child select a set of red blocks to equal a set of blue blocks—on his own.

- Take a specific number of toothpicks, buttons, paper clips, etc. and arrange them in different patterns:

Ask him if they are the same number. (Eventually he concentrates on the number of units within a set rather than on the arrangement of those units or the total space they occupy. We say that he has achieved *conservation of number*—discussed in the case of Ruthie in this chapter. This means that three apples, three pencils, three pennies will always be three in number and that this number will always be attached to a group of three objects.)

- Combining sets: partial counting, or "counting on." At a lower level, give a child a pair of dice, have him count the dots on the first die, and continue to count through the dots on the second die, knowing that the last number means how many in all.

$$(. .)$$
At the next stage, when he sees ( ) he says "four;" and seeing (. . .)
$$(. .)$$
he counts, "five, six, seven. Seven in all."

While some children will move smoothly with school instruction into $4 + 3 = 7$, others will not, continuing to count from one.

$$(. .)$$
An intermediate procedure is substituting the digit 4 for ( ) but
$$(. .)$$
keeping the pattern (. . .) so that the child begins with "4," then counts the dots to 7.

At that point he should be asked to say the *whole sentence* out loud: "Four plus three is seven." (Whenever possible in beginning a new procedure, a child should be encouraged to do, see, and say all actions simultaneously; later to see and say.)

Learning to add and subtract

- Practice with concrete materials; use pennies, buttons, etc.; *Cuisenaire rods*, Cuisenaire Co. of America, Inc., 12 Church St., New Rochelle, N.Y. 10805; *Uni-fix*, Diday Educational Resources, 3 Dearborn Rd., Peabody, Mass. 01960; snap-beads (child's toy).

- Subtraction is a particular stumbling block. Make the idea of "take away" meaningful by physically removing two cookies from a dish of five cookies. Some learning-disabled children do not understand that removing the two cookies represents subtraction because they know that the cookies are still in the room. They have to be shown dramatically that the cookies have been *definitely* removed. Perhaps the cookies will have to be eaten to prove the point.

  Concrete materials make arithmetic meaningful for children. Handling and manipulating them helps the youngsters to understand numbers and sets. They are used in the early stages of new learning. Once a child is more sure of himself, he will transfer motor activities to mental acts, and eventually to paper and pencil tasks. For the learning-disabled child the change from motor to mental acts is more of a hurdle. He will need more practice with concrete materials for a longer period of time.

Techniques for Specific Problems in Math

Poor auditory recall

To remember number names, write them, say them, associate them with the corresponding number of objects in a picture.

To learn number names, use a deck of cards. Do simple matching or play card games. For learning and teaching through card games, refer to *Deal Me In*, by Margery Golick (Jeffrey Norton Publishers, Inc., 145 East 49th Street, New York, N.Y. 10017). The card games, such as Blitz and Solitaire, described in Golick's book teach and reinforce in a pleasurable way many basic skills—sequencing, directionality, and motor skills as well as number concepts.

TO LEARN NUMBER FACTS

1. Use flash cards.

2. Verbalize facts: "Two plus three equals five"; "Three times four equals twelve."

3. Make your own lotto game: For example, each player has a card with numbers which represent answers to addition problems. One player calls out a problem, for instance $4 + 7$. Each player who has 11 can cover that square. The one who fills his card first wins.

6	9	8
4	11	3
2	7	5

You can make lotto cards with subtraction, multiplication, and division answers.

4. Use a number line for addition and subtraction:

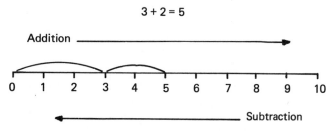

$3 + 2 = 5$

5. Give the student a multiplication chart to use:

0	1	2	3	4	5	6	7	8	9	10	11	12
1	1	2	3	4	5	6	7	8	9	10	11	12
2	2	4	6	8	10	12	14	16	18	20	22	24
3	3	6	9	12	15	18	21	24	27	30	33	36
4	4	8	12	16	20	24	28	32	36	40	44	48
5	5	10	15	20	25	30	35	40	45	50	55	60
6	6	12	18	24	30	36	42	(48)	54	60	66	72
7	7	14	21	28	35	42	49	56	63	70	77	84
8	8	16	24	32	40	48	56	64	72	80	88	96
9	9	18	27	36	45	54	63	72	81	90	99	108
10	10	20	30	40	50	60	70	80	90	100	110	120
11	11	22	33	44	55	66	77	88	99	110	121	132
12	12	24	36	48	60	72	84	96	108	120	132	144

To multiply—Find the number you want to multiply on the left side of the chart (6, for example) and the other number on the top (8). Move straight across the chart to the right from the number on the left (6) and straight down from the number on the top (8). The number at which they meet (48) is the answer.

6. To learn and practice multiplication facts, a gridiron produced by Child Guidance, Inc. may help and is available in toy stores.

7. Have the child bounce a ball as he says his facts, such as: 2, 4, 6, 8, 10; 3, 6, 9, 12; etc.

8. Play *Domino Addition.*[1] Prepare this set of domino cards:

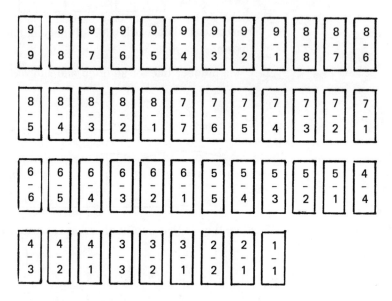

ADDITION SOLITAIRE

Shuffle the cards (or dominoes). Deal out the entire set in ten stacks face up. Five of the stacks will have five cards each and five will have four cards each. Ten cards will be showing at a time until the last part of the game.

Remove cards in *pairs* so that the sum of the four numbers named on the two cards is 20. If one of the stacks is entirely removed, break a remaining stack into two in any way (without looking at the cards) and restore the setup to ten stacks.

The player wins against the deck if play continues until one card is left. That card will have a sum of 10 if all of the play is done correctly. If no combination of 20 is possible at any time, the deck is the winner.

For variation, if the player is winning too infrequently, increase the number of stacks to eleven or twelve. This makes winning easier. If the player needs greater challenge, decrease the number of stacks to nine or eight.

Another format that plays out entirely is to remove three cards whose sum is 30. In this case, no cards will be left in the case of the player winning. It is also self-correcting because of this fact.

[1]Lola May, *Addition and Multiplication Domino*, The Winnetka Public School System, Winnetka, Ill. 60093. Directions for two games have been included here. Lola May has devised other games using this same set of cards.

ADDITION COMPETITION

Shuffle the cards. Deal five cards to each player and place five cards in a vertical line on the table. A player may place any card to the left of one of the five cards on the table if the player's card has a sum one less than the table card. If the sum on the player's card is one more than on a table card, a player places it to the right of the table card. For example, the sum of 12 could be played to the left of the $^9/_4$ card and the sum of 14 could be played to the right. Similarly, the sum of 6 could be played to the left of the $^6/_1$ card and the sum of 8 to its right. As the cards are built to the left, the sum must always decrease by one. To the right, it must always increase by one. The rows can be as long as necessary. Each player plays exactly one card per turn. If no card in hand can be played, cards are drawn from the bone pile until a play is possible. The object is to get rid of the five cards or all cards in hand.

9. Use the following multiplication game[2] based on a puzzle technique: The game consists of keys and a solution pie. Each key has a problem on it and the grooves in the key fit the grooves to the answer in the pie. Ask the child to find the right key to the right answer; it will fit the key on the pie. Examples of keys to this pie include:

$$4 \times 4 = 16 \qquad 3 \times 3 = 9$$
$$8 \times 2 = 16 \qquad 9 \times 1 = 9$$

(Note that two keys will fit the grooves to the same answer if their products are the same—for example, 6×4, 3×8.)

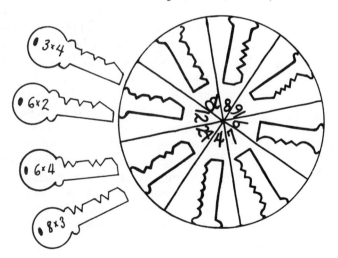

Different solution pies and keys can be made for addition, subtraction, and division as well as for further multiplication problems.

---

[2]Devised by Jocelyn Eichler, New Rochelle, N.Y.

10. For practice, use *Look into the Facts*, Creative Publications, Inc., P.O. Box 10328, Palo Alto, Ca. 94303. (Book 1: Addition and Subtraction; Book 2: Multiplication and Division.) There is a *Teacher's Guide* for these books.

In a column of addition, if a child cannot hold in mind several facts at once, have him write down each step:

$$
\begin{array}{ccc}
3 & & \\
] & \text{is} & 9 \\
6 & & \\
\underline{+\,5} & & \underline{+\,5}
\end{array}
$$

Poor sequencing

TO LEARN NUMBERS IN ORDER

1. Scatter the numbers 1 through 10 from a deck of cards on the table; have the child put them in order.
2. Play card games, like solitaire.
3. Count, using a number line.
4. Play board games, like *Parchesi* and *Uncle Wiggly*.
5. Play Addition Competition.

TO COUNT BACKWARDS

1. Draw a number line on the floor with chalk: have the child march from 10 back to 1, counting as he goes.
2. On a ruler or a number line, move a marker or an index card backwards; have the child count each number out loud as you show it.
3. Increase the difficulty of the task by placing a marker on the target number. Going backward from 10 to 1, have the child look at 10, say 9 which is covered, then look at 9, say 8 which is covered, and so on. As she responds, immediately uncover the target number to inform her of the correctness of her response.
4. Race the calculator—Have the child start with a number on the calculator, 12 for instance. Ask him to subtract 1 on the calculator and try to respond (11) before it does. Have him continue to subtract 1 each time until he reaches 0. Be sure he checks his answers with the display on the calculator, each time.

To skip count, by 2, 5, 10. For example, by 5: at an early stage, have the child whisper *1, 2, 3, 4,* say *5* out loud; whisper *6, 7, 8, 9,* say *10* out loud, and so on. To do a multi-step problem list each step in sequence for the student to follow. He should use the list as a crutch until he learns the procedure—what to do first, second, third.

When numbers and their names differ

If a child has difficulty reading and writing numbers whose names are not written the way the numbers are spoken, have her verbalize what she hears and sees:

> 14: hear fourteen; see one four (not 41)
>
> 32: hear thirty-two; see three, two (not 302)

Left-right orientation

Use the same methods used in overcoming directionality problems in reading and writing numbers to tackle directionality problems in math.

Language problems

To understand the language of math, terms must be fully explained:

1. Often concrete examples are necessary; have the child arrange objects, such as boxes, graduated in size, in order. Label them so that while she manipulates them, she can learn words such as small, smaller, smallest, big, bigger, biggest.

2. To illustrate *more* than or *less* than, draw a ladder, number the rungs and place the terms *more* or *less*, as pictured:

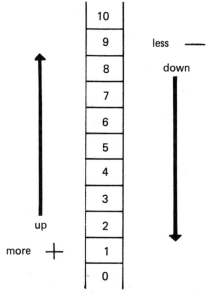

On the ladder, you can teach the child the meaning of *more* (going up) and *less* (going down). The ladder can also be used, like a number line, for counting, addition, and subtraction.

3. To establish concepts of *before* and *after:* Deal one-third of a deck of

cards to the child and one-third to yourself. From the remaining pile, take a card and place it face up on the table (an 8, for example). The child takes a card from his pile. If the number comes just *before* the 8 (7) or just *after* the 8 (9), he captures it. Have the child say, "Seven comes *before* eight," or "Nine comes *after* eight," as he takes the card. The players take turns trying to capture the card placed in the center of the table.

The child must learn that different words can mean the same thing. Use different expressions to say the same thing so the child becomes familiar with the terms. For example, in subtraction, the terms *remain* and *left*:

> "*If you take eight pencils away from eleven pencils, how many are left?*"
> "*If you take eight pencils away from eleven pencils, how many remain?*"

To help a student with problem-solving skills, have him use the following as a guide:

a. Look at the problem as a whole.
b. Answer the question, "What are you to find?"
c. Determine what facts you are given to work with.
d. Select those facts that are essential.
e. Decide on the process to use.
f. Estimate the answer.
g. Compute the answer.
h. Compare it with the estimated answer. Does the answer make sense?

Spatial awareness

To improve poor spatial judgment, give a child many trials with concrete materials. For example, he will require more practice than other children combining the correct number of rods to equal a rod of a given length:

Use the Cuisenaire Geoboard (Cuisenaire Company of N. America, 12 Church St., New Rochelle, N.Y. 10805).

Visual perception

To help a child recognize the positions of numbers on a number line, do the following:

1. Draw a large number line. Take a piece of string and ask the child to place it between 3 and 8, for example. Then cut the piece of string

that lies between 3 and 8. Do the same thing between 4 and 8. Have him compare the pieces of cut string and see that the distance from 4 to 8 is shorter, and therefore, 4 is closer to 8 than 3 is to 8.

2. Using a large number line, the above idea can be demonstrated by using dried beans or peas. A child will see that there are fewer beans between 4 and 8 than between 3 and 8, and realize that 4 is closer to 8 than 3 is to 8.

Disalignment

For children who cannot align their numbers correctly for computation:

1. Use graph paper:

		3	2	5
		×	1	4
	1	3	0	0
	3	2	5	
	4	5	5	0

			2	8
			3	5
		+	6	1
		1	2	4

2. Fold a piece of ordinary lined paper vertically in columns. Opened, it can be used like a piece of graph paper (horizontal lines being the original lines, vertical lines being the folded lines) to help a student keep his numbers in the correct columns.

Poor Visual-Spatial Memory

To help a child transfer between horizontal and vertical forms of the same problem:

1. Use a magnetic board. Have the child set up and do a problem both ways. For example,

$$5 + 2 = 7 \qquad \begin{array}{r} 5 \\ + 2 \\ \hline 7 \end{array}$$

2. Have the child set up and do problems vertically and horizontally with wooden or plastic numbers.

Visual rotation

If a student is troubled by perceiving the difference in signs, such as + and ×, emphasize to him that he must learn to look at all signs *very carefully*. To distinguish between the signs that confuse him, tracing and writing them, and describing his movements out loud ("straight down," "straight across,") might help.

For seeing the difference between the division and subtraction signs, have the child use different colors for the dots of the division sign.

Children come up with interesting devices on their own. For example, one boy could only remember the multiplication sign by crossing his fingers.

Math Operations

For learning-disabled students, generally the traditional approach, where each process is structured and taught in a simple, direct way, is successful. Many new concepts are too complicated for the learning-disabled student.

Highly recommended is *The Rauen Math Dictionary*, by James J. Rauen—James Rauen, Box 1711, Los Gatos, Ca. 95030. This book explains very clearly step-by-step operations that use the traditional as well as new math methods.

MATH OPERATIONS AND COMPUTATION

Basic math operations all depend on sequencing backwards and forwards and comprehending part–whole relationships. Also, understanding that for every action that takes place there is another action that undoes it is basic to the concept of numbers: $2 + 2 = 4$, $4 - 2 = 2$; $4 \times 4 = 16$, $16 \div 4 = 4$. Piaget refers to this as a sense of reversibility which a child must develop in order to compute.

The four basic math operations using computation are addition, subtraction, multiplication, and division. Computation is based on counting. When we add, we count forward. When we count backward, we subtract. When we count forward in any number group, we are multiplying: $4 + 4 + 4 + 4 = 16$, which is the same as $4 \times 4 = 16$. When we count backwards in any number group, we are dividing:

$$
\begin{array}{r}
16 \\
- \ \ 4 \\
\hline
12 \\
- \ \ 4 \\
\hline
8 \\
- \ \ 4 \\
\hline
4
\end{array}
$$

This produces the same result as $4\overline{)16}$.

While many of the learning-disabled can understand these operations, computation is another matter. Because computation presents such an obstacle due to language and visual-spatial problems, we feel that learning-disabled children learn better and faster with traditional math.

Some phases of the new math are helpful. However, many aspects of it are too much for these students, such as advanced vocabulary and concepts, early use of equations, focus on analysis (expanded notation), and self-discovery. If learning-disabled students are weak in math, they generally do not learn through self-discovery. Math is too abstract for them. *The Rauen Math Dictionary*, already referred to, is an excellent self-help book for high school students and adults not too severely handicapped in math. Also, this book is a guide for teachers, parents, grandparents, and volunteers who are teaching and reinforcing basic math skills from fifth grade on. (Some parts can be used in the lower grades.) A person does not have to be a math whiz to teach arithmetic skills if he has a book like this.

Basic skills for computation can be learned. Many people who are troubled by math in the early grades lose confidence in themselves and become frightened by it. They try to stay clear of anything to do with arithmetic. But this is an impossibility in our world today. Even young children go to a store and have to make change. They spend their allowances, buy lunch in the school cafeteria, and so on. Later on as adults they write a check, figure out take-home pay, pay taxes, make a budget, and so forth. For those who need practical math, there are many books on the market, some of which are:

Arithmetic Skilltext in Daily Living, Workbooks A,B,C, Special Service Supply, Box 705, Huntington, N.Y. 11745.

Arithmetic That We Need, Frank E. Richards Publishing Co., Phoenix, N.Y. 13135.

Math That Pays Off, Pal Practical Living Series, Xerox Education Publications, Columbus, Ohio 43216.

The Money You Spend, Turner Livingston Series, Follett Publishing Co., Chicago, Ill. 60606.

Scoring High in Math, Random House, Inc., New York, N.Y. 10022.

Scoring High in Survival Reading: Earning and Spending, Random House, Inc., New York, N.Y. 10022.

Using Money Series, Frank E. Richards Publishing Co., Phoenix, N.Y. 13135.

Counting My Money

Making My Money Chart

Buying Power

Earning, Spending and Saving

MATERIALS SUGGESTED

Arithmetic Handbook, Michael Parkis, Ann Arbor Publishers, Inc., Naples, Fla. 33940.

Cues and Signals in Math, Kitty Wehrli, Programmer, Ann Arbor Publishers, Inc., Naples, Fla. 33940.

Cuisenaire Rods, Cuisenaire Company of N. America, 12 Church St., New Rochelle, N.Y. 10805 (See catalogue for additional materials)

Data Man Calculator, calculator and manual, Texas Instruments Inc., Lubbock, Tx. 79408.

Decimals and Percentages, Frances Fein Loose, Ann Arbor Publishers, Inc., Naples, Fla. 33940.

Essential Modern Mathematics, A–D, Ginn and Company, Boston, Mass. 02117.

Fractions One and Two, Frances Fein Loose, Ann Arbor Publishers, Inc., Naples, Fla. 33940.

Improving Your Ability in Mathematics, Harcourt Brace Jovanovich, New York, N.Y. 10017.

Look Into The Facts (four operations), Creative Publications, P.O. Box 10328, Palo Alto, Ca. 94303.

Michigan Arithmetic Program, Kitty Wehrli, Programmer, Ann Arbor Publishers, Inc., Naples, Fla. 33940.

Numbers For You and Me, Malcolm E. Mellott and Dan T. Dawson, Prentice-Hall, Inc., Englewood Cliffs, N.J. 07632.

The Rauen Math Dictionary, James J. Rauen, Box 1711, Los Gatos, Ca. 95030.

Reading For Mathematics, Joyce Friedland, Irene Gross, Frank E. Richards Publishing Co., Phoenix, N.Y. 13135.

Steps in Mathematics, Steck-Vaughan Co., Austin, Tx. 78767.

Uni-Fix Rods, Didax Educational Resources, 3 Dearborn Rd., Peabody, Mass. 01960. (See catalogue for additional materials)

Useful Arithmetic, Vols. I and II, Frank E. Richards Publishing Co., Phoenix, N.Y. 13135.

For Basic Competency

Meeting Basic Competencies in Mathematics, Dr. Eileen L. Corcoran, Frank E. Richards Publishing Co., Phoenix, N.Y. 13135.

Michigan Prescriptive Program in Math—High School Equivalency, Dr. William E. Lockhart, Ann Arbor Publishers, Inc., Naples, Fla. 33940.

8 WRITING AND SPELLING

WRITING

In the last few years, the schools have been emphasizing the importance of knowing how to write—having the ability to express one's thoughts in written form. This aspect of teaching has been neglected for a long time. As a result, too many high school and college students, and adults, find this form of expression difficult. To express thoughts in writing is not easy for most people—for students writing a composition, for businessmen writing a report, for authors writing a book. Writing is a complex subject that involves organization of thought, sound usage of the English language, and imagination. In addition, if there are difficulties in handwriting and spelling, problems in composition can be compounded.

Some children seem to be born with a flair for writing. As soon as they are able to print, they are composing little stories and poems, enjoying writing letters and keeping diaries. Jill, a ten-year-old, is a child like this. The following is one of her short compositions:

> *I'll never forget Gathedrill Gourge I went to. It was very beautiful and interesting. The only thing I won't forget is the way the ice frooze around the trees and made like an ice sculpture. Another beautiful attraction was the sizes and shapes of the iceacles which hung from the rocks. The iceacles looked to me like spears. When they fell we went to get them so we could lick them. Some of them froze beautifly. A few had curly swervy lines almost like engraved in the ice. I hope*

everyone gets to have the experience I had at Ashokan where all these things took place.

Jill described her impressions and feelings in an imaginative, mature way for her age. Yet there is much for her to learn if she expects to become a good writer. She must begin by improving her spelling and phrasing. Because she delights in creative writing, she may dislike research papers. She will need to discipline herself. If in later years Jill chooses to become a professional writer, then she will discover that drawing on her own experiences and pondering on their meanings will be the core of her best writing. Mastering the mechanics of composition will become easier for Jill with time and experience. Nevertheless, she will realize, as most authors do, that well-written expression of mature ideas always requires reflection and involves hard work.

Competent writing *is* hard work. However, in time, most children learn to write sentences, paragraphs, and compositions. It is difficult to generalize about expectations in the field of writing because writing is an individualized aptitude. Moreover, this skill depends significantly on the type of teaching a student receives. Naturally, the student must master the basics of syntax and learn to conform to the disciplines of various types of writing. Nevertheless, students and adults will do better if they have the opportunity to write about subjects that are meaningful to them. Not every student is creative like Jill and turned on by beautiful icicles. Some may be more interested in describing an exciting marathon race or a moon landing. Some may be reluctant to write and may need special motivation.

Reading and writing are taught simultaneously. After a schoolchild has learned to read a certain number of words, he can write sentences independently. Just as there are stages in learning to read, there are sequential steps in learning to write.

The Main Steps in Writing

DEVELOPING A SENTENCE

Start by writing a short, simple sentence, then gradually expand it by adding words that make the sentence more meaningful:

The girl jumps.
The girl jumps rope.
The little girl jumps rope.
The little girl jumps rope during recess.
The little girl jumps rope during recess in the schoolyard.

A sentence usually consists of the following features: (1) It is a group of words that expresses a complete thought; (2) it starts with a capital letter; (3)

it ends with a period, question mark, or exclamation point; (4) it has a subject and a predicate; (5) it can be structured as a simple, compound, or complex sentence. Sentence structure is linked to the study of grammar. (See "Understanding Sentences" in Chapter 6 and refer to grammar books listed at the end of this section.)

CONSTRUCTING A PARAGRAPH

A description of an average paragraph will include the following: (1) It is made up of a group of sentences that are related to one topic; (2) it contains a topic sentence which expresses the main thought, followed by supporting details; (3) it is indented at the beginning.

The child starts by composing simple paragraphs—for example:

My family likes sports, My brother
plays tennis. My sister swims. My
parents jog.

Students begin writing longer and more involved paragraphs as they move along in elementary school. By the time they are in junior high they have learned that paragraphs are generally organized into three parts: the beginning, or introduction (often the topic sentence); the middle or development; and the end or conclusion.

In junior or senior high school, students learn to organize topics according to what is being discussed.

1. They learn to use the same patterns in writing that they have encountered in reading; time order, cause and effect, comparison–contrast, and arbitrary listing (for examples, see pp. 171–172).

2. They learn to make use of signal words, met in reading, as transitional words in writing to connect and introduce new thoughts. These words may be used to join sentences or paragraphs. Examples: *however, moreover, because,* etc. (For signal words, see p. 172.)

WRITING A COMPOSITION

Whereas a paragraph consists of a group of related sentences, a composition is formed by a group of related paragraphs, generally organized in three parts: introduction, discussion (the longest part), and conclusion. There are different types of composition:

narration—an account based on the writer's experience or imagination.

exposition—an explanation about people, ideas, situations using detailed facts and examples.

argumentation—a discussion in which the writer justifies an opinion.

description—a verbal picture that tells about a person, place, or thing.

PLANNING A PAPER

Just as a competent reader inspects an author's plan before beginning a chapter or book, a successful writer makes a plan before composing a well-thought-out paragraph or composition.

Organizing one's thoughts into outline form is the best way to plan. For example, if a ninth-grader is asked to write a short paper on the characteristics of Scarlett O'Hara, he approaches his assignment in the following way: First, he jots down at random all the ideas that come to mind about Scarlett. Next, he groups ideas that are related to each other and then finds a topic under which to classify each group. In the case of Scarlett, he notices that some of the qualities listed were admirable; others were not. So he decides that his main headings will be simply *good* qualities and *bad* qualities. He then is ready to make the following outline:

CHARACTERISTICS OF SCARLETT O'HARA

I. Good Qualities
   A. Courageous
      1. Saved Tara
      2. _____
   B. _____
      1. _____
      2. _____

II. Bad Qualities
   A. Unscrupulous
      1. Tried to take Ashley from Melanie
         a. _____
         b. _____
      2. _____
   B. _____
      1. _____
      2. _____

This form is more or less standard and can be applied to most types of advanced writing. For a more complex research paper, notes and note cards can be grouped and classified to support the main points.

PREPARING AND COMPLETING A PAPER

Write a rough draft following the outline
Make corrections in usage
Find specific and colorful words
Add and delete phrases and sentences where necessary
Rewrite awkward paragraphs

Write the final copy

Edit for mistakes

In establishing good writing skills, considerable practice is needed to progress from the simple sentence to the long composition. When working with a student, determine the stage he has reached in his writing skills, and begin teaching at that point.

Many intelligent, verbal learning-disabled students may have grave difficulties with written expression. These are attributable to various problems—poor syntax, disorganization, inability to sequence ideas, and immature writing. In addition, they may have trouble expressing abstract ideas in written form. Often their writing is severely impeded by labored handwriting and poor spelling.

Children with severe writing disorders embracing many of the aforementioned problems often produce unintelligible writing. The following is an example of the jumbled writing nine-year-old Teddy produced:

When I want always dive a car. I been thing ever sents. Now I whon to own a ming bike.

When asked to interpret what he wrote, he said:

"When I was little, I wanted to drive a car and I've been thinking ever since. Now I want to own a mini bike."

Techniques to Improve Writing

For the person who thinks very quickly, but whose hand cannot keep up with his thoughts:

1. Ask him to verbalize his thoughts in a simple sentence before writing. Start by posing a question which requires a simple written answer. For example, in Teddy's first tutoring session, he was asked: "What do you take when you go mountain climbing?" He said, then wrote:
   When I go mountain climbing, I take a pack, raingear, lunch and something to drink.
2. If possible tell him to put a story on tape, speaking very slowly. Have him listen to it and then write it down. If he is older, he can type it.
3. Ask him to dictate a story to you, leaving the ending for him to write. This technique is particularly effective for the person whose difficulty in composition is compounded by handwriting problems.

For the person who lacks ideas and/or resists writing—the following techniques can be used for anyone needing practice in writing.

1. Use puppets in a variety of ways:

- A child can give a puppet show, then write down the dialogue.
- A child can pretend a puppet is a newscaster reporting a ball game, then write down his comments.
- A child can have two puppets discuss why they dislike writing, then write down their remarks.
- A child can have a puppet describe the best meal he ever had, then write down what he ate.

2. Ask a youngster to think of the five senses and write what he *dislikes* to taste, smell, hear, feel, see. (Use one complete sentence for each sense.)

3. Ask a child to write what she *likes* to taste, smell, hear, feel, see—using complete sentences.

4. Give a youngster a story starter. For example, begin a tale about two boys who ran away from home and were caught in a storm; have him write the ending.

5. Suggest interesting topics to write about:
   - What do you keep under your bed?
   - What's in mother's pocketbook?
   - The silliest present I ever had.
   - What did you do when the train broke down?

6. Have the student write a character sketch about an acquaintance, describing his appearance, his work, his hobbies, his likes, his dislikes.

7. Use newspaper articles; ask the student to write her own headlines.

8. Use pictures for subjects of stories. Gear them to the student's interest. For example, after showing him the picture of the purse-snatching in Chapter 3, ask him to be a witness to the crime and report what he saw, in writing.

9. Give the older student more provocative material on which to write. Ask her to comment on an editorial. Does she agree with the writer? Ask her to discuss current topics, such as problems with the environment, the death penalty, the draft, health foods.

For the person who needs structure and organization:

1. Refer to "Main Steps in Writing" earlier in this chapter for structuring sentences, paragraphs, and compositions. The learning-disabled child or adult may need extra practice at each stage.

2. Use comic strips from the newspaper. After the child reads the strip, ask him to write a short story about it, keeping the ideas in order.

3. An additional exercise which is enjoyed by the young child, but which can also be used with older students, involves writing a paragraph on

how to do or make something with which he is familiar. For example:

- How to make brownies
- How to repair a bicycle tire
- How to make a paper bag puppet

For the person who needs to make his writing more interesting, colorful, and effective, instruct him how to:

1. Vary the beginnings of sentences. Don't start all sentences with the subject. Use prepositional and participial phrases, adverbs, adjectival and adverbial clauses at the beginning. For example:

   (subject first) Julie waited for Jack's phone call.

   (adverb first) Anxiously, Julie waited for Jack's phone call.

   (prepositional phrase first) For over two hours, Julie waited for Jack's phone call.

   (participial phrase first) Waiting anxiously for Jack's phone call, Julie was impatient.

   Give the student a sentence starting with a subject; ask him to vary its beginning.

2. Use specific and more graphic words. Practice using the thesaurus or dictionary to find more precise words as replacements for common words like *sad, excited*, etc. Can the student find more specific words to replace overworked words?

   said (yelled, announced, whispered)

   things (clothes, equipment, belongings)

   walk (hasten, amble, stroll)

   Give the student a sentence using a common word. Ask him to replace it with a word that is more explicit. For example:

   Last Saturday, the boys walked *through the green forest. (hiked for walked)*

   "Look out! Pat is about to fall off his tricycle," said *Molly. (screamed for said)*

   Ask the student to substitute more precise words for phrases using *very:*

   very *happy* (ecstatic)

   very *slow* (labored)

   very *uncertain* (vague)

3. Vary sentence length. Paragraphs become less monotonous if there is difference in the lengths of sentences.

4. Use figurative language to arouse feeling and imagination. A good figure of speech may spark an idea. For a discussion of different types of figures of speech and teaching techniques, see Chapter 4.

5. Use transitional words, such as *first, second, since, when, moreover,* to achieve unity in paragraphs and compositions, to bridge one idea to another. For transitional words, see Chapter 10.

6. Make use of the five senses to stimulate ideas for writing. This is especially effective with students who tend to be literal. For instance, if a student has recently been at a football game, ask him what he heard, saw, smelled, touched, felt while he was there. His impressions can serve as the basis for a short description. Use this same technique with any situation that is familiar and interesting to a student, such as the cafeteria at school, a garage sale, a boat ride.

Carrie was a child who had difficulty expressing her feelings. With frequent practice using her senses, she was able to write the following piece about Christmas:

> *On Xmas morning I sit in my bed and listen to all of the sounds outside. I hear the rushing water and the wind blowing in the forest because I have Xmas in the mountains. When I get up I run into the living room and call, "Merry Christmas," so that every one will wake up. Then I dive into the presents. After all the presents are opened my mother cooks the bacon and eggs. They smell so good. Xmas is my favorite holiday.*

7. Use paraphrasing (restating an author's ideas into one's own words) to promote facility in expressing just what a prose passage or poem means in simple clear language. A middle school student might be given a verse of "Casey At The Bat" by Ernest Lawrence Thayer to paraphrase:

> *It looked extremely rocky for the Mudville nine that day;*
> *The score stood four to six, with but an inning left to play.*
> *So, when Cooney died at first, and Burrows did the same,*
> *A pallor wreathed the features of the patrons of the game.*[1]

High school students studying Shakespeare are asked to clarify the intent of obscure passages in his plays. This type of paraphrasing is generally difficult because it involves interpreting more figurative language.

> *All the world's a stage,*
> *And all the men and women merely players:*
> *They have their exits and their entrances;*
> *And one man in his time plays many parts,*
> *His acts being seven ages.*
>
> AS YOU LIKE IT
> (WILLIAM SHAKESPEARE)

All types of paraphrasing help develop vocabulary and the precise use of words, and are an excellent foundation for writing summaries.

---

[1] Ernest Lawrence Thayer, "Casey At The Bat," as quoted by Paul Witty, Miriam E. Peterson, Alfred E. Parker, *Reading Roundup, Book I* (Boston: D.C. Heath & Co., 1954), p. 211.

The literal learning-disabled students who have difficulty with the connotations of words have problems learning to paraphrase. They have to ponder before realizing that "The teacher left the room" and "The teacher went out of the room" have the same meaning. They need practice in using synonyms and rewording phrases before moving on to more complicated material. For example:

Chicken pox is easily spread among children

Chicken pox is contagious

For practice in paraphrasing, use *Increasing Reading Efficiency* by Lyle Miller (New York: Holt, Rinehart & Winston, 1970).

Common pitfalls for all students

PARALLEL STRUCTURE

My sister likes swimming, tennis, and to go sailing. (incorrect)

My sister likes swimming, tennis, and sailing. (correct)

RUN-ON SENTENCES

At the theater I realized I forgot my tickets the ticket agent gave me a receipt. (incorrect)

At the theater I realized I forgot my tickets. The ticket agent gave me a receipt. (correct)

MISPLACED MODIFIERS

Sandra bought a necklace at the jewelry store with her initials on it. (incorrect)

Sandra bought a necklace with her initials on it at the jewelry store. (correct)

PROBLEMS OF PRONOUNS

My parents do not like me watching too much television (incorrect)

My parents do not like my watching too much television. (correct)

He expects Sam and I to clean the garage. (incorrect)

He expects Sam and me to clean the garage. (correct)

PROBLEMS OF AGREEMENT

A pile of books were left on the desk. (incorrect)

A pile of books was left on the desk. (correct)

These are only a few examples of difficulties students have with correct usage. Double negatives, confusion between adjectives and adverbs, problems of verb tenses, dangling constructions and superfluous words must also be tackled. Students must be able first, to recognize mistakes in usage, and second, to avoid them in their own writing. They must practice applying what they learn in their own paragraphs and compositions.

If good writing is such a demanding task for the achieving student, think how frustrating it must be for the highly intelligent, verbal, and creative youngster impeded by severe disorders in written expression. His or her impediment must be comparable to that of an adult stroke victim who retains his mental faculties but loses his ability to talk except in gobbledygook phrases.

Such a thwarted boy was Terry, a learning-disabled high school student. The following is an example of his writing before remediation.

> *A person who wants to be accepted by a group or certain persons may dress accordingly. also may to do the opposite to show their rejection of a group of persons. A person who doesn't care about others in rejection or about themselves either will probably not maintain a very clean, groomed appearance.*
>
> *It is my opinion that in light of how much appearance can influence associability and keeping a friendly image which involves relations it is wise to have a groomed so called healthy appearance.*

Two and a half years later, after working winter and summer on written expression, Terry was able to write the following:

> *Far off in the distance beyond all our realities lies the world of our fantasies. Staring off into the infinite we think as we are suspended in space drifting in our thoughts of tomorrow and yesterday. Where are we going to? Where am I now? I wonder where it all began, where it will end. Wisps of images blow before my mind. All the endlessness of space and of time are combined into a void of my dreams.*

An exceptionally gifted boy, Terry was able to overcome his writing problems, mainly because of his persistence and willingness to keep plugging away. He wished to write. He wanted to express ideas. He succeeded.

MATERIALS SUGGESTED

For the Younger Child

Building Sentences Step by Step (word/phrase cards), by Dorothy MacCarr, Dormac, Inc., Beaverton, Ore. 97075.

Creative Writing Activities, Walter B. Barbe, Ph.D., Highlights for Children, Inc., Columbus, Ohio 43216.

Imagine and Write Series, grades 2–6, My Weekly Reader Books & Teaching Aids, Xerox Education Publications, Columbus, Ohio 43216.

Language Arts Sampler, Curriculum Associates, North Billerica, Mass. 01862.

Pencil Power (composition and handwriting), My Weekly Reader and Teaching Aids, Xerox Education Publications, Columbus, Ohio 43216.

Writing Power Series, grades 3–6, My Weekly Reader Books and Teaching Aids, Xerox Education Publications, Columbus, Ohio 43216.

For the Older Student

Awareness: Exercises in Basic Composition Skills, Suanne Maca and Dorothy Patterson, Xerox College Publishing, Lexington, Mass.

Composition, Books I, II, III, Sara Hickman, Educators Publishing Service, Inc., Cambridge, Mass. 02138.

English: A Comprehensive Course, Harold Levine, AMSCO School Publications, New York, N.Y. 10013.

Improving Composition through Sentence Study of Grammar and Usage (for high school and college), Carol Crompton, Educators Publishing Service, Inc., Cambridge, Mass. 02138.

Paragraph Practice (Junior High–Adult), Kathleen E. Sullivan, Macmillan, Inc., New York, N.Y.

The Paragraph, Carolyn Smith, Educators Publishing Service, Inc., Cambridge, Mass. 02138.

Patterns: Reading for Composition, James D. Lester, William C. Brown Co., Dubuque, Iowa.

Sense of Sentences, Wilbert J. Levy, AMSCO School Publications, New York, N.Y. 10013.

Today: A Text-Workbook for English Language and Composition, Hans P. Guth, editor, Webster Division, McGraw-Hill Book Company, New York, N.Y.

Vocabulary and Composition, Harold Levine, AMSCO School Publications, New York, N.Y. 10013.

SPELLING

a witch is a spuk she goes spuking peple on halloween.
On halloween nite she went to spuk evrybutey.
but in sted a girl spuked her.

(8-YEAR-OLD GIRL)

Sadat and Bagin were courages men. They forgot ideas of vengence and became peaceable. After they signed the framework for peace they both new that there would be meny troublesome argument in the future. The judgement of most people was that Carters position was adventageious for his future in politics.

(31-YEAR-OLD MAN)

There is an old saying that some people are born spellers; but realistically, spelling does not come naturally to most of us because of the inconsistencies in the English language. Some find it easier than others to learn to spell.

Competent readers may or may not have spelling problems. However, poor readers often have difficulty spelling. Readiness skills for spelling are similar to those for reading, except that written spelling also involves handwriting. Severe difficulty in handwriting also impedes spelling, so, if a child is handicapped in this way, be sure to check his oral spelling. In many instances, it may be adequate or very good.

All the problems that hinder progress in reading can affect an individual's spelling, such as:

Poor visual memory: He spells everything phonetically—*thay* for they, *sez* for says.

Auditory problems: He cannot hear sounds—writes *putten* for button, *pen* for pin.

Sequencing, ordering: He makes reversals—*siad* for said, *baot* for boat.

Leaves out letters: He writes *prefence* for preference.

Leaves off endings: He writes *ship* for shipped.

Techniques for Spelling

Be sure to give a few trials when introducing a technique to the student, to determine if it works. In most cases, he or she will need to practice the new procedure several times before meeting with success. In general, a student needs continual practice and reinforcement to improve spelling.

Learning through phonics

When we teach phonics, we are simultaneously teaching spelling. Starting with beginning phonics, you can see how spelling skills are developed. Spelling and phonics work in tandem, so that a child can be taught spelling where words can be broken down and reconstructed phonetically. The child who has trouble spelling entire words will have less difficulty with individual syllables and will be able to arrange the parts of words correctly.

With just the sounds of letters a child has learned, you can ask him:

What do you hear at the beginning of the word *mat*? (m) Write the sound you hear: m __

What do you hear at the end of the word *fun*? (n) Write it: __ n

What do you hear in the middle of the word *cat*? (a) Write it: __a__

If the child can do these tasks, he is ready to write and to spell *man*.

Another exercise that combines phonics and spelling requires the child to fill in the missing letter when you say a sentence.

"Jan sat on a mat."

J—n s—t on a m—t.

or "Jim hit with a bat."

J—m h—t with a b—t.

As a child proceeds through a phonics program, he also continues to focus on spelling. Four-letter words like *land* and *jump* follow the simpler ones cited above.

Spelling can be aided by tackling words in parts. When a child begins to analyze words in terms of their prefixes and simple endings, he can also practice putting them together, spelling them:

re set, help ing, un lock

Looking at words and their parts involves syllabication. In spelling, the child hears the syllables, spells each syllable, puts the syllables together.

hab it   sun set

(For rules of syllabication, see pp. 85–86.)

Many spelling problems can be avoided if the student carefully says the word that he wants to spell, listening for each syllable. (If he needs practice hearing syllables, he should clap or tap each one as he says it.) Why is *lit er a ture* sometimes spelled *literture* or *litrature*? The speller may have heard only three syllables.

Learning through visual memory

Spelling also depends on a good visual memory. Many words do not have standard phonetic elements, and often the same sound can be represented in numerous ways—for example, the *long i* sound: pipe, cry, high, buy, isle.

Have the student copy the word he wants to learn; look at it carefully; cover it up, then see if he can spell it from memory. Copy the word to be spelled on paper; trace it; have him close his eyes and write it in the air with his finger. Then, have him try to write it correctly. (In closing his eyes, he is eliminating any distraction and concentrating solely on the word.) This technique, referred to as skywriting, is an aid to spelling words which *must* be learned visually. It is particularly helpful for those who have a weak visual memory.

Learning through auditory memory

Have the student look at a word; then have him spell the word orally, listening carefully to himself; then have him write it down.

Learning through grouping

Group words with similar sounds and spelling together for learning, such as the following:

rain   loud
pain   cloud
pail   found
trail   ground
wait

Learning through the kinesthetic method

The following approaches, used for teaching reading, will also help improve spelling when children have problems with both sight words and phonics.

1. Write a word on the child's back; have him copy it on the board.
2. Have the child feel letters made from pipe cleaners, window sealer, or sandpaper, that make a word. Then see if she can write it down.
3. Spell a word in his hand; see if he can write it down.
4. Spell the word on her forearm; ask her to write it down.
5. To practice spelling, use *Anagrams* or *Link Letters*, produced by Milton Bradley, Springfield, Mass., available in toy stores.

Learning through rules and generalizations

Correct spelling can be aided by rules. The person who can conceptualize will find rules particularly helpful. This approach works well with learning-disabled students. Some of the most important generalizations include:

1. The possessive case of a noun always has an apostrophe. In possessive singulars, the apostrophe comes before the *s: farmer's, country's.* In possessive plurals, the apostrophe comes after the *s* if the plural ends in an *s: weeks', boys'.* The apostrophe comes *before* the *s* if the plural does *not* end in an *s*: men's, children's. The possessive pronouns *its, hers, theirs, ours, yours,* never have an apostrophe.

2. Put *i* before *e* except after *c* or when sounded like *a* in *neighbor* or *weigh: i* before *e*—believe, mischievous; *ei* after *c*—perceive, receipt; *ei* = *a*—weigh, eight. Some exceptions are *foreigner, leisure, seize, height, neither,* and *weird.*

3. If a word ends in silent *e*, it usually drops the *e* before adding a suffix beginning with a vowel: *hope—hoping, use—usage.* Do not drop the *e* if the ending begins with a consonant: *nineteen, safety.*

4. Words ending in *y* preceded by a consonant change *y* to *i* before any suffix except one beginning with *i: cry—cries, hurry—hurried.* An exception occurs with suffixes beginning with *i: crying, hurrying.*

5. If a word of one syllable ends in a consonant and is preceded by a single

vowel, double the final consonant before adding a suffix beginning with a vowel: *bat—batting, plan—planned.* Do not double the final consonant before adding an ending if a word ends in two consonants: *mend—mending, last—lasted;* or if a word has two vowels before the final consonant: *feed—feeding, heat—heated.*

6. Words of more than one syllable, in which the last syllable ends in a consonant preceded by a vowel, double the final consonant before adding a suffix beginning with a vowel *if the last syllable is accented: admit—admitting, prefer—preferred.* If the last syllable is *not* accented, do *not* double the consonant: *limit—limiting, gallop—galloped.*

Learning-disabled children with severe spelling problems rarely become good spellers, but they can be helped to improve. Others who have less difficulty will learn to spell fairly well with hard work and a good dictionary.

Spelling books we have found especially useful with learning-disabled students include the following.

MATERIALS SUGGESTED

Workbooks and Programs

Dr. Spello, William Kottmeyer, McGraw-Hill Book Company, Inc., New York, N.Y.

Goals in Spelling, 1–7, William Kottmeyer and Kay Ware, Webster Publishing Co., Manchester, Mo. 63011.

Magic Squares, Sally B. Childs, Ralph de S. Childs, Educators Publishing Service, Inc., Cambridge, Mass. 02138.

Power Over Words, Hetty P. Archer, Clista M.E. Dow, Educators Publishing Service, Inc., Cambridge, Mass. 02138.

Spell of Words, Elsie T. Rak, Educators Publishing Service, Inc., Cambridge, Mass. 02138.

Spellbound, Elsie T. Rak, Educators Publishing Service, Inc., Cambridge, Mass. 02138.

A Spelling Workbook for Corrective Drill for Elementary Grades, Mildred B. Plunkett, Educators Publishing Service, Inc., Cambridge, Mass. 02138.

A Spelling Workbook for Early Primary Corrective Work, I, IA and II, Mildred B. Plunkett, Caroline Z. Peck, Educators Publishing Service, Inc., Cambridge, Mass. 02138.

Spelling Your Way to Success, Barrons Educational Services, Woodbury, N.Y. 11797.

Dictionaries

The Bad Speller's Dictionary, Random House, Inc., New York, N.Y.

Instant Spelling Dictionary, Career Institute, 1500 Cardinal Drive, Little Falls, N.J. 07424.

Games

Scrabble, Selchow and Richter Company, New York, N.Y. 10010.

Spill and Spell, Childcraft, New York, N.Y.

⑨ HANDWRITING

Fine handwriting is a skill to be admired, but it is not a requisite today. Nevertheless, children have to write legibly, easily, and fairly quickly in order to cope in school. Adults who lack this skill will be able to function in the business and professional world only if they have a good secretary or learn to type. Pity the pharmacist who has to read a doctor's scribbled prescription or the secretary who has to decipher a lawyer's messy affidavit. We must be able to express our thoughts in writing if we are to communicate with others in letters and papers and with ourselves in taking notes. Of course, some of us are more skillful than others in this area. Moreover, many children who are highly verbal when it comes to oral expression have great difficulty with handwriting, which in turn limits their written expression.

For many years, schools that had remedial programs for learning-disabled children focused primarily on reading. This was natural—learning to read comes first, then spelling, and finally handwriting and composition. Schools now include the latter two subjects in their learning-disability programs.

Printing is taught in the first two grades, and cursive writing, or script, is generally started in the third grade. Some special-education people prefer teaching only cursive writing to learning-disabled children. They feel cursive writing helps these children because it is more rhythmic, and keeps them going in one direction, thereby avoiding reversals. Not everyone agrees with this theory and some think printing is easier. Some educators have found that joining printed letters is easier for many disabled writers.

Just as there are variations in all learning abilities and disabilities, as we pointed out in Chapter 2, there are extreme differences in handwriting, a grapho-motor skill. Disabilities in this area range from mild to severe. The following samples will show these variations:[1]

Come to my garden
In spring time and hear.
Birds singing sweetly

Come to my garden
in spring time and hear
Birds singing sweetly
& summer is near

Come to my garden.
In spring

Come to my garden
in spring

---

[1]Items 4, 5, and 6 from the *Metropolitan Primary Cursive Handwriting Scale* by Gertrude H. Hildreth, published by The World Book Co. Reproduced by permission. Copyright © 1930 Metropolitan Achievement Tests, Primary-Handwriting. Renewed by Harcourt Brace Jovanovich, Inc. All rights reserved.

To simplify the complex subject of handwriting we will describe four varying groups of writing dysfunctions and then illustrate teaching techniques.

BRAIN-DAMAGED

Some children who have been brain-damaged by accident or disease will show very poor coordination. They cannot combine movements; they and jerky and arythmic and seem to "jitterbug on paper." They cannot grip their pencil correctly. These children are very difficult to teach and some need special schooling by trained professionals.

CHILDREN WITH A MODERATE DISORDER

These children's problems are not as severe as those of the first group, but they have a definite writing disorder. Their writing is very slow and labored and is barely legible. Peter, a gifted reader with an I.Q. of 145, was an example of a boy in this group. Although he spoke fluently, he had great difficulty forming his letters. He could write only a few words and short sentences. After several years of working on his handwriting, he still had great problems with assignments of any length.

CHILDREN WITH MILD PENMANSHIP PROBLEMS

The children in this group do not have a writing disorder like those in the second group, but their penmanship is extremely sloppy. They exhibit the same tendencies as children with more severe handicaps. Many of them are very bright and their thoughts outpace their ability to express themselves in writing. They race ahead, not taking time to write legibly. They could write legibly if they slowed down. Some children who have no handwriting problems write too rapidly because of anxiety.

LEFTIES TRAINED LIKE RIGHTIES

Children in this group frequently write poorly and fatigue easily.

DIFFERENT METHODS
OF TEACHING HANDWRITING

Many learning-disabled children in these groups have poor muscle coordination and have difficulty forming letters. For the most part, they are not ready for writing instruction when they enter school.

There are readiness skills for writing that are similar to those necessary for reading. These include discrimination of shapes, letters, and sounds, memory for letter shapes, and association of sound and symbol. Writing a word is a complex task. Think of Robert, who is just learning to write. In addition to the skills just mentioned, he will need fine motor coordination to print a letter. He will also need the ability to remember what the letters look like, how the letters are formed, what direction they go in, and how to space them. Moreover, when he learns to spell, he will have to remember the sounds of the letters.

In teaching skills involving motor coordination, we move from gross to specific motions. We must start the teaching of handwriting with large arm movements because these children do not have the ability to use small wrist movements. The following sequential steps will help a child develop handwriting.

Getting Ready to Write

1. On a large surface (chalkboard or a table covered with newsprint), have the child make designs with her *whole arm* using magic markers or chalk. Choose designs that are components of letters and numbers:

-for o, a, d, g

-for m, n, h

-for u, w

-for 6

2. Do this task on a large piece of paper or chalkboard. Ask the child to put his elbows to his sides and to use his forearm to practice drawing horizontal and vertical lines, which are the ingredients of printed letters:

for L H T F I

for M N Y X
V W Z

3. When the child is ready to use his wrists, ask him to draw small circles going in both directions: ◯ ◯ ◯   ◯ ◯ ◯

Writing Letters

1. Ask the child to start making the letters formed by circles and half circles—*o a c:* ◯ ◌ ◖

The following charts[2] illustrate the starting point and direction required for the proper formation of letters:

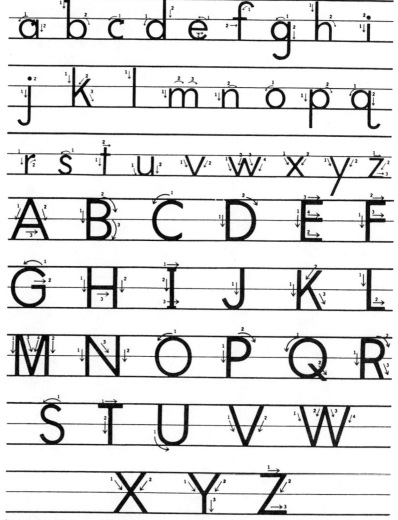

[2]From *Readiness for Learning* by Pierce H. McLeod, published by J.B. Lippincott Company; copyright © 1973, 1965. Reprinted by permission of the publisher.

2. Instruction is easier if certain letters and numbers are grouped together. For instance:

circle letters and numbers: *o c a g d 0 9*

small letters beginning with a line: *m n r*

tall letters beginning with a line: *l t h b k*

letters with slanting lines: k v w x y z

numbers with curves: 6 8 3 5

3. Of primary importance is showing the child the starting point of a letter
and the direction in which he should move his pencil.

Cursive Writing

Cursive writing is taught in the same systematic way as printing, going from
large movements to small, from large designs down to small ones. It is also
important to give a child the starting point and direction of the strokes. In
cursive writing the rhythmic swing is necessary for forming the letters
correctly. It is good practice to join the manuscript letters together to
develop smooth writing. For reference: Right Hand Alphabet.[3]

[3]Elsie T. Rak, *The Spell of Words* (Cambridge, Mass.: Educators Publishing Service, 1970).

In teaching writing, follow one program and stay with it. Excellent writing programs include: Warren T. Johnson, *The Johnson Handwriting Program* (Cambridge, Mass.: Educators Publishing Service, 1976–77); Helene C. Dubrow, *Learning to Write, Book I*, and *Learning to Write, Book II, Swing Into Letters* (Cambridge, Mass.: Educators Publishing Service, 1968).

The Lefty

A lefty can be trained as easily as a righty as long as he or she is not forced into a writing program intended for right-handed students. This type of program, which is counter to the child's natural directional dominance, often leads to nervous tension, fatigue, and frustration. A left-handed person should position his paper in the opposite direction from a right-handed person and should hold his pencil an inch or inch and a half from the point, so his vision is not blocked.

When he begins to write, a thick fountain pen with a fairly blunt point is preferable to a ball-point pen. A lefty generally writes in a backhand slant. To help him maintain directional consistency, he can use paper with slanted lines. Sometimes guidelines at the top of a paper or a card at the side of the paper is all that is necessary. (A few lefties position the paper vertically and write accordingly. If they are more comfortable this way and their writing is more legible, their writing habits should not be changed.) For reference: Left Hand Alphabet.[4]

[4]Rak, *The Spell of Words.*

Programs of help for the left-handed person include: Mildred B. Plunkett, *A Writing Manual for Teaching the Left-Handed* (Cambridge, Mass.: Educators Publishing Service, 1967), and Dorothy Emerson, *Help Yourself to Better Handwriting* (Cambridge, Mass.: Educators Publishing Service, 1954)—For left- and right-handed.

Other Problems That Hinder Good Writing

1. Poor pencil grip.

2. Poor writing position. Where children have been working in open classrooms and open spaces, positioning may have been neglected. They may not have been shown the proper writing position; they may have been writing on floors or on walls.

3. Spatial problems:
   - Letters do not stay on the line
   - Letters are not formed in the correct position
   - Letters and words are incorrectly spaced; they are either too far apart or too close together
   - Words spill over into the margin

4. Trouble with direction of letters; reversing b and d, inverting n and u. Many children and even adults have difficulty remembering that a letter never changes its position, and if it does, it becomes another letter— reverse the b and get d, invert the n and get u.

5. Poor motor memory—inability to remember how to form the letters. This problem is similar to the one a person has when he cannot remember which way to turn the wheel of a car while backing into a parking space.

Techniques to Cope with These Handwriting Problems

To correct a poor pencil grip

For an older person, unlearning this habit is very hard. If he finds the change too difficult, he should not try to make it. Demonstrate the correct grip; show the child how to hold the pencil.

Have the child write with large crayons and thick pencils, or attach a commercial gripper to an average-size pencil or twist a rubber band near the point of the pencil.

To correct poor writing position

The proper position must be acquired. Demonstrate the correct position of the body, arm, and hand with the correct slant of the paper.

For the righty: For the lefty:

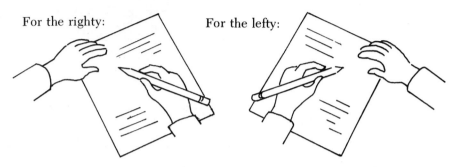

To cope with spatial problems

If the child has difficulty staying on the line, make a heavy line (black or red) on the line on which he is writing so he *sees* where the letters should rest:

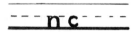

Cut out a window in a piece of cardboard. Place the bottom inside on the line on which the child is writing so he can *feel* where the letters should rest:

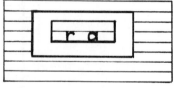

If he cannot form his letters in the correct position, above or below the line, give him a paper with colored lines and have him practice individual letters:

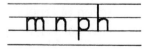

If he has difficulty spacing his letters and words, have him write individual letters in squares and words in boxes:

In all writing tasks, show the child in which space parts of the letters should be written. Have him place his finger between each word he is writing. (This will help him whether his letters are too close or too far apart.)

Have him write his name on graduated labels or his address on graduated envelopes, to help him judge space.

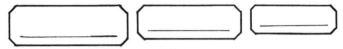

Have him write numbers and letters in squares of large graph paper. This may be done to the timing of a metronome, which many children enjoy, but some dislike.

If the child spills over into the margin while writing sentences or compositions, darken the margin with a heavy black or colored marker.

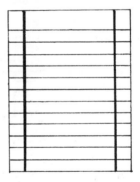

To establish correct direction of letters

Make a letter out of pipe cleaners, felt, or clay. Have the child feel the raised letter, close his eyes and trace the letter while saying its name, then write the letter down.

Have the child trace the letter with his finger on the table, close his eyes, write it in the air, then write it down. (Try having him write it down with his eyes closed, then with them opened.)

Have the child face the blackboard. Write a letter on his back with your finger. Have him write it on the board.

Write a letter in the palm of the child's hand. Have him write it on the board.

To develop motor memory

A child may recognize all the letters of the alphabet and know them by their names and sounds. However, when he wants to write them down without a copy, he forgets how to make them. He creates his own version.

Choose a systematic approach to handwriting.

Tackle a few letters at a time.

Focus on where the letters start and in which direction the letters go.

Use the tactile methods mentioned previously if the child learns well through the sense of touch.

Do a lot of tracing of letters; continually show the child the direction in which to make them.

When poor motor memory for forming letters is the cause of a severe handwriting disorder, the problem is often not recognized. Roly-poly twinkly-eyed Scotty had this misfortune. An intelligent, creative, spoiled nine-year-old, he had as much difficulty printing as a kindergartner. The school psychologist and remedial specialist took it for granted that Scotty's struggle with writing letters, which he could easily recognize and name, was caused by extremely poor muscle coordination. As a result, Scotty spent much time in school copying designs and doing exercises to strengthen fine motor skills. Diagnosis outside of school, however, indicated that Scotty's fine motor skills were excellent; he could copy designs and letters accurately, and, in addition, could draw and paint very well. In short, Scotty was a talented embryonic artist, but he was hampered by an inability to recall how to form the different letters.

Difficulties with handwriting can have emotional effects. Great effort is needed to improve handwriting, and children who have a persistent drive to succeed are, of course, the most successful in overcoming their difficulties. Written assignments can be unsurmountable burdens, and the problem worsens in the upper grades. Children who are not capable of writing long compositions often falter after a few burdensome paragraphs. They fall apart at the seams; sentence structure, punctuation, and writing ability all fly out the window and their papers become messy and illegible. When required to recopy a messy paper, they produce an even more horrendous one. They are being asked to do the impossible.

In the past, parents and teachers were not aware of this and thought the youngsters were lazy or stupid. When Eddie's mother was given an explanation of his handwriting problem, tears came to her eyes. She thought he was just lazy. "I should have guessed something was wrong," she said, "for no matter how many times I made him recopy a paper, he always made more mistakes and became sloppier, and we always ended up screaming at each other."

Like Eddie's mother, many teachers in the past thought that untidy papers were the result of laziness and carelessness. Now most know that they should limit writing demands on these children and allow them to make oral or taped reports. Tutors working with these children and parents should communicate with classroom teachers about curtailing assignments. They should see that their students with handwriting problems take a typing course. Some older children prefer printing, and this should be allowed if it is easier for them. Boys and girls incapable of taking notes should be encouraged to bring a tape recorder to class. Older children especially are very ashamed when they have to hand in sloppily written assignments. Tutors and teachers should be accepting of their difficulties and try to bolster their self-confidence.

10 LEARNING PROBLEMS OF ADOLESCENTS

"How was your first day of junior high school?" asked Dan's mother. In his usual manner of speaking, Dan answered in clipped phrases: "Giant school—there were three floors, too many halls, rooms and turns. And we had that blackout; it would have been hard enough with lights. Couldn't concentrate. Nothing was well organized. Many schedules were messed up; everyone told you to go to someone else for help. Nothing was made clear!"

When a child leaves his small neighborhood elementary school and enters a traditional junior high, he is stepping into another world. Gone is the friendly, structured atmosphere and the close supervision that gives him a sense of security. Gone are the teachers who knew him since kindergarten. Perhaps in the upper elementary grades he left his homeroom for several classes, but work was well coordinated by the teachers.

Adjusting to a large new school is difficult for almost all children, but most learn to cope and are mature enough to handle the situation. Not so the learning-disabled child, who is mainstreamed for most of his classes. He is confused by the noise and bustle in the hallways; his poor sense of spatial orientation and directionality makes finding his way to distant classrooms a grim adventure. Additionally, the whole atmosphere is more stressful, and these children often miss the support and individual attention they received in the elementary schools. Only in recent years have the middle schools and high schools been giving more attention to youngsters with learning problems. Many junior and senior high schools have learning

163

disabilities specialists and resource rooms, where students are taught in very small groups. There generally is not enough time for much individual instruction, unless there are teachers' aides and supervised volunteers to lend a hand.

Many guidance counselors are knowledgeable and extremely helpful, alerting teachers to individual problems. However, secondary school teachers are frequently overloaded and need to be reminded to modify programs or obtain easier textbooks for the learning-disabled child. So parents and anyone working with such a child should keep abreast of the situation.

Most standard textbooks are too difficult for the learning-disabled youngster, so it is vital to find books at his particular level. Furthermore, a problem for these boys and girls may arise when a teacher eliminates textbooks, compiles his own material, and teaches through dictation. He may also have the students copy from the board, which may be too time-consuming, and study sometimes from overcrowded, often illegible mimeographed sheets. If a pupil with learning problems is being taught this way, a parent or tutor should obtain the teacher's plan of work or materials, and suggest that the student take a tape recorder to class if one is available.

Starting in seventh grade, the work-expectancy level becomes more demanding. Schools in different areas vary so much that it is hard to generalize on the standard of work. However, just as there are readiness skills for first grade, there are readiness skills for junior high school.

What abilities does a boy or girl need to tackle junior high work? Of primary importance, his mechanics of reading, writing, and spelling must be fairly automatic. When it comes to reading, the main focus is on comprehension. His vocabulary must be fairly extensive and his understanding of the different connotations of words and figurative language must be at a high level. During these years students will learn to read critically, to judge literary quality and to discriminate among many types of writing. They will learn to recognize the difference between comic book humor and the witticisms of Mark Twain, between a sensational romance and a beautiful love story like *Romeo and Juliet*. As future voters and consumers, they must learn to analyze television and radio commentaries, newspaper editorials, and advertisements. This means they must be able to check facts for accuracy and distinguish between arguments and slanted propaganda. All these skills must be refined throughout junior and senior high.

Most students are able to cope adequately with the curriculum. Unfortunately, there are some who run into trouble. There are always youngsters, who may be bright, who coast through elementary school with a minimum of effort. They never really become committed to education since their main interests are nonacademic. In junior high they require help in developing needed skills. With this help, many of these youngsters settle down, become self-motivated, and progress rapidly. Others for many reasons become frustrated and resistant to any type of aid offered. They need expert handling to avoid school failure and pitfalls, such as truancy and problems with drugs and drinking.

It is important to find out if any of the boys and girls in this latter group are learning-disabled youngsters. Sometimes they are, and if a student has been diagnosed as learning-disabled and given an understanding of his school problems, he feels better about himself. For him, appropriate remediation often leads to success.

As one might expect, the learning-disabled children who have been contending with learning problems since their early years will still require special help in junior high. Generally they lack certain phonics skills or have difficulty with vocabulary, grammar, and composition.

In addition, there is another group of boys and girls who may need special attention and support. These are the youngsters who had learning problems in the early grades and seemingly overcame their difficulties in elementary school. For them, junior high seems to turn back the clock. The workload, long reading assignments, and the pressure of added demands often cause old problems to resurface.

Bobby was a success story by the end of fourth grade. Everyone had worried about him—his parents, his grandparents, and his teachers. He had struggled in learning to read and needed special help in and out of school. Bobby's determination and willingness to work, combined with good remediation, won out; by the time he was in fifth grade, he was reading at grade level and achieving good grades. Best of all, he was able to work independently—no more tutors, no more resource room.

He sailed into junior high with confidence—but it was not long before he floundered. Old problems reappeared in reading and writing when he tried to complete long assignments too quickly. Moreover, his comprehension suffered. He became so frustrated and anxious that any organization skills he had learned vanished. Bobby needed help again.

Individual tutoring involved reviewing phonics, improving his rate of reading, and emphasizing study skills. Most students will not have to focus on relearning basic skills. However, like Bobby, they will need continued work on vocabulary and comprehension (see Chapter 6), and will benefit from learning good study skills.

RATE OF READING

As the boy or girl progresses in school, an extremely slow reading rate can be a handicap, especially in junior high school, high school, and college. Completing lengthy reading assignments is an impossibility for many students, and the resulting frustration engenders a defeatist attitude. "Why try?" they ask.

Fortunately, we can help most children and adults improve their rate; we can help some more than others, depending on the causes of the individual's slow reading. Let us take a look at different groups of students who read too slowly.

1. The word-by-word reader: he pronounces each word that he reads either out loud or to himself. This is a difficult habit to break if it continues too long.

2. The perfectionist: even though he is not a word-by-word reader, his pace is naturally slow. He is afraid to miss anything.

3. The learning-disabled student with residual problems in word attack skills: he cannot read very quickly because he is forced too often to figure out unknown words. Even though some learning-disabled students become adept at structural analysis (or breaking down words into their parts), they may fatigue easily when overloaded with homework. They, too, end up reading at a slower rate. If learning-disabled boys and girls attempt to read too quickly, their old reversal problems and other perceptual difficulties resurface. Consequently, their comprehension also suffers. In addition, their focusing problems can interfere with rate of reading.

4. Individuals can have a mixture of problems, including:

   Poor concentration—inability to keep one's mind on the subject.

   Impulsivity—a tendency to do everything too rapidly, including reading. These rapid readers, even though usually intelligent, have poor comprehension because they should be reading at a slower rate. In reality, many of them are very slow readers.

   Slow grasp of main ideas and weak vocabulary.

   Poor visual memory. When reading, students with poor visual memory have to look back frequently to recall what they have read.

   Disinterest in reading. Students with limited reading experience have never had a chance to build up a good rate of reading.

WHAT SHOULD YOUR RATE OF READING BE?

Rate of reading should be related to purpose and its effectiveness should be judged by comprehension.

1. If you are reading for pleasure and not required to remember what you read, move at a good pace. You can be a speed reader.

2. If you are reading a history textbook, mathematical, scientific, or technical material, which requires full understanding and recall, read carefully, which means you must read slowly and accurately. Following

directions and interpreting complicated subject matter also demand thorough reading. Speed reading simply does not work.

3. If you are looking for particular information—for example, a date or a certain fact—or trying to get the general idea of a book, skim. This is the kind of reading in which your eyes glance rapidly over the page searching for significant words and phrases. Skimming is often combined with thorough reading. When doing a research paper, first skim for pertinent material, then read selected parts carefully.

4. There is no one answer to the question, "What is the average rate of reading?" An efficient high school or college reader, reading easy material at 500 words per minute, might have to slow down to 250 words per minute when reading a difficult book. Likewise, a junior high school student who reads some material at 275 words per minute might have to slow down to 150 words per minute when presented with more complex work.

Techniques to Improve Rate of Reading

1. To overcome vocalizing (saying each word as you read it), have the student hold a pencil between his teeth or chew gum when he reads. At the same time, suggest that he practice reading in word groups.

2. Explain to the student that the normal wide eye-span makes it possible to read word groups or phrases instead of reading word by word. Reading in phrases is more efficient. Show a student that he has a wide eye-span: Ask him to hold his index finger up about a foot from his face; ask him to look at it directly and tell you what he sees on either side of his finger. He will be able to see objects on either side.

    When a student is reading orally, suddenly cover up the last few words at the end of the line. The student will be surprised to discover that he can say the words that follow because he has already read them. This shows him that he can see a few words at a time.

    When a student is reading orally, tell him to look up from the page at intervals, continuing to verbalize what he has seen. Poetry is good material because the lines are often short and easy to recall.

3. Reading in correct thought groups, prepositional phrases, clauses, descriptive phrases, is one of the most important skills for improving rate of reading and comprehension. During the transition from oral reading to silent reading in the early grades, reading in thought units should be emphasized.

    Have the youngster group thought units in the following manner:
    The baby robin / fell out of the nest / in the high tree / onto the ground.

Ask the youngster to read a phrase and choose *all* possible phrases that could make a meaningful sentence:

I went on a train . . .

in the water   over the fence   to visit my family   *under the stove*   along the river   *wherever you go   through the clouds*   which was traveling fast   *under the bed.*

Suggest that the student practice reading in phrases with easy material. Newspaper and magazine articles written in columns are good items for this purpose.

Motivate easy reading for pleasure. This is perhaps the most helpful way to improve rate of reading.

4. Explain to the student that not every word is important in reading. Use a telegram to illustrate the point. Paul sent the following telegram:

Excited great news lead role Broadway production Our Town

He knew that every word cost money so he was careful to choose only the necessary words, omitting the unimportant ones. Nevertheless, he conveyed the message as well as if he had written it out completely:

I was excited to hear the great news that I have the lead role in the Broadway production of Our Town.

In preparing the student to focus on important words and to pass over unimportant ones in reading, give him a lengthy sentence to write in the form of a telegram. Do this a few times.

Next, choose a few paragraphs for him to read. Ask him to underline the meaningful words in each sentence.

Finally, have him read paragraphs without underlining. He should try to read as fast as possible, making his eyes move from one important word to the next.

5. Have the student practice timed readings. Many timed readings can be found in anthologies used in English classes and in workbooks used in reading centers and resource rooms. For example, *Reader's Digest Skill Builders*, Grades 3 and up (Reader's Digest Services, Inc., Pleasantville, N.Y.) or *Timed Readings*, Edward Spargo and Glenn R. Williston (Jamestown Publishers, Providence, R.I.).

Suggest the student keep a home reading chart. Tell him to set the same time for reading the same book each night. Ask him to record the number of pages he covers at each sitting. See if he can push himself to read faster.

Methods which involve timing, such as those just mentioned, generally create too much pressure on the learning-disabled child. Timed reading with this type of youngster should be avoided unless requested. Because of their many-faceted problems, learning-disabled students should not be expected to read at a rapid rate.

20 Minutes	Name of Book _____		
	Number of Pages Read		
	1st week	2nd week	3rd week
Monday			
Tuesday			
Wednesday			
Thursday			
Friday			
Saturday			
Sunday			

HOW TO READ AN ASSIGNMENT

Many years ago Ruth Strang described how a student could become a more efficient reader. She pointed out that previewing an article, chapter, or book cuts down on reading time, and reviewing it immediately helps the student retain what he has read. Her formula for this is SQ3R, which stands for survey, question, read, review, recite.[1] This approach has been adopted by many educators and has been presented in different ways. Students have found the following steps for reading an assignment useful.

1. Look over the book or chapter before reading.

   In a book, skim the table of contents to get the author's plan through the chapter headings.

   In a chapter or article, note the boldface type headings.

   Skim the first and last chapter of a book or the first and last paragraph of a chapter quickly to get the general idea. Generally the introduction presents and the conclusion summarizes the main points of a chapter succinctly.

   Note charts and illustrations.

   Note the title; sometimes it is informative.

2. Read with questions in your mind.

   As you read, let the teacher's questions guide you in locating information required for the course.

[1] Adapted from Ruth Strang, *Study Types of Reading Exercises* (New York: Teachers College Press of Teachers College, Columbia University). Copyright © 1951 by Ruth Strang. All rights reserved.

Before reading a chapter, if there are questions at the end, refer to the questions. They point up the most important ideas and details in the chapter.

As you read, turn any boldface type headings into questions. They will direct your reading. For example: "The Abolition Movement Drives North and South Apart" as a question might become, "How did the abolition movement drive the North and the South apart?"

3. Review what you have read. Upon completion of reading, close the book and *immediately* try to recall what you have read by saying it out loud. This will help you remember. If there are important points you have forgotten, check back.

4. Reviewing for a test means more than just rereading. You must organize different material in various forms for study—depending on subject matter and course requirements. For instance, you may need to classify scientific data or compare the characteristics of two chemicals; you may have to trace the events leading to the climax of a short story or book, or interpret the actions of the main character. As for history, you may use the following specific plan for reviewing any historical period:[2]

a. Conditions at beginning

b. Causes of change

c. Incidents of change—dates

d. Important people

e. Results of change

f. Significance to world

Once you have organized the material to be reviewed, ask yourself questions which could be on the test, and answer them. Do this on a tape recorder if one is available. Listening to your answers will give added reinforcement to memory.

AIDS TO MEMORY

There are some people whose auditory memory is comparable to a recording machine; they can remember almost word for word what they hear. There are others who have a photographic memory and can remember what they see on a page, practically word for word. These people are the exceptions. For most of us, memory requires considerable concentration and effort. How much we get out of a course or how well we do on a test depends to an extent on good memory. This can be developed by:

[2]Adapted from Rachel Salisbury, *Better Work Habits* (Chicago: Scott, Foresman & Company, 1932) p. 197.

1. Concentrating
   - Focusing on the material
   - Finding a quiet place to study—taking regular breaks
   - Avoiding distractions
   - Not letting your mind wander (Pick other times to daydream)

2. Understanding
   - Getting the overall picture of what you are trying to remember before you tackle it, part by part—for example, hearing the whole song before memorizing it line by line, or reviewing the whole experiment in science before remembering it step by step in sequence.
   - Grasping the meaning—the more meaningful the material is to you, the better you will remember it

3. Reviewing what you have learned at intervals spaced further and further apart.

4. Using all your senses—hearing, seeing, writing—will reinforce memory.

5. Using a mnemonic device—an association you make up to help you remember. For example, you can remember two s's in *dessert* because you want more. There is only one s in *desert;* one desert is enough.

IDENTIFYING PATTERNS IN READING

Writers and speakers arrange and present their ideas in different ways, different patterns. There are four common patterns: time order, cause and effect, comparison and contrast, arbitrary listing. Writers also select signal words as clues to help readers recognize which patterns they are using. Learning that signal words indicate dissimilar patterns aids the reader or listener in identifying them. This will help him comprehend more quickly what he is studying. Therefore, practice in spotting patterns is recommended.

The following are examples of designs in writing and speaking. The signal words are in boldface.

1. Time Order—Pattern in which the student can recognize the sequence of events or the steps in a process.

   The day started out badly for Mrs. Ames, the substitute teacher. **First,** *she had trouble quieting the noisy children and calling the class to order.* **Then,** *a small boy in the rear started to throw spitballs.* **After** *she had sent him from the room, everything was more peaceful.* **Finally,** *Mrs. Ames was able to take the roll call.*

2. Cause and Effect—Pattern in which the reader or listener identifies causes and results.

*After the close of the Civil War in the United States, President Lincoln wanted to help the impoverished and devastated southern states. He advocated a lenient policy for their readmittance into the Union. **Because** of his assassination, politicians with different ideas came into power. **As a result,** the South was treated harshly and Congress passed the Reconstruction Acts, which were bitterly resented by the Southerners.*

3. Comparison and Contrast—Pattern in which the student can see likenesses and differences among people, situations, and ideas.

*If you take a bus ride in Jakarta, an important city in Indonesia, you will be in for surprises. **On the one hand,** you will be impressed by the main street, a wide boulevard flanked on either side by beautiful modern buildings housing important banks from all over the world. **On the other hand,** you will be shocked when your bus turns off the main street. You will be driving on narrow dirt lanes flanked by open sewers and miserable shacks.*

4. Arbitrary Listing—Pattern in which the reader or listener is presented with a group of facts or thoughts whose arrangement can be arbitrary.

*There are many types of automobiles on the market. **Some** are extremely large and high powered, like the Cadillac and Lincoln Continental. **Others** are medium-sized (called compacts), like the Oldsmobile Cutlass and the Ford Fairmont. **Another** type of car, perhaps the most popular of all, is the very small four-cylinder foreign car like the Volkswagen, and the American-made small car like the Chevette.*

Examples of signal words and phrases used in different patterns:

1. Time Order: first, second, then, not long after, at last, finally, later, next, after a short interval
2. Comparison and Contrast: on the one hand, on the other hand, but, however, on the contrary, yet
3. Cause and Effect: as a result, for this reason, because, consequently, on that account, since, although
4. Arbitrary Listing: in addition to, also, another, some, others, furthermore, besides, moreover

While most writers and speakers use signal words, sometimes they are omitted. In these cases, the student is expected to follow the steps of the author's thinking on his own. It is more difficult to read or listen without signals. Previous practice using signal words will help the reader or listener identify the pattern even without clues.

NOTE-TAKING AND OUTLINING

Once a student can see patterns, note-taking becomes much easier, and his notes become more meaningful. For a student who has problems taking notes, practice in recognizing patterns will be particularly helpful. He can name causes, list results; he can separate likenesses and differences and make comparisons; he can put experiments in the right order. Then, more formally, he can organize his notes into a useful outline for studying. There are many types of outlines but they generally have the same form. The following paragraph has been outlined to illustrate the standard form.

The penguins have an unusual family life. After the female lays an egg, she leaves. The male is responsible for hatching the egg. Egg hatching takes two months. When the new chick comes out of his shell, he is fed by the father. Later, the mother penguin returns and she and her mate raise the young penguin together.

I. Penguins have unusual family life
   A. Female lays egg and leaves
   B. Male responsible for hatching egg
   C. Egg hatches in two months
   D. New chick fed by father
   E. Mother returns
   F. Both parents raise young penguin

This paragraph was done according to time order. Other outlines can be based on causes, problems, results, likenesses, differences, characteristics, and so on. Some examples of possible subjects: *Causes of the Industrial Revolution, Results of World War II, Similarities and Differences between John Steinbeck and Charles Dickens, Advantages and Disadvantages of the Marshall Plan, Characteristics of Scarlett O'Hara.* Outlining helps an individual remember and study what he has read. It also will help him prepare for writing.

TEACHING ADOLESCENTS WITH LEARNING PROBLEMS

Teaching underachieving teenagers is challenging and complex. Not only do you have to fill in the gaps and remediate residual problems, but you must help them cope with daily classwork. In other words, they must be helped to catch up and keep up. Nevertheless, in some ways adolescents are easier to teach than younger children. At this age they have a background of living experiences. Many of them have settled down and have developed some strategy for coping in difficult areas. High school students also realize that they will be on their own in a few years. They become more realistic and self-motivated.

Adolescents are struggling for independence, and when pressured by parents and teachers, may become provocative in school and resist academic work. Many of those with learning problems have been burdened by years of struggling and have a low self-image. Frustrated and frightened, they may become discouraged and resentful when placed in remedial classes. Some drop out of school. Many operate by denial. Anxiety impedes learning, so the first task in teaching is to reduce apprehensiveness. Giving these students insight into their problems and developing competence in their weak skills pave the way to success. It may help them if you explain that a number of famous people, like Winston Churchill, Woodrow Wilson, and Nelson Rockefeller, as well as Albert Einstein and Thomas Edison, mentioned in Chapter 1, had learning problems.

Many weak students are extremely talented in art, music, sports, mechanics, acting, or writing. These talents should be encouraged; the focus should not be only on the deficit areas.

Consider the case of Allen, a charmer whose big blue eyes and soft curly hair beguiled many teachers. Being intelligent, he was able to slide through elementary school with passing grades. It was not until junior high that his undetected learning problems caught up with him. He started to fail his major subjects and became so frustrated that he did not bother to hand in his assignments.

On the recommendation of the school, he was given a psycho-educational evaluation. Results indicated that Allen was an extremely verbal youngster with superior abstract ability who had compensated for many early learning disabilities. On the other hand, he still had residual problems, due to developmental lags, which impeded his academic functioning and induced feelings of inadequacy. Some of the problems that required remediation included confusion of blends (such as *fr* with *thr*), omission of syllables in spelling, and written expression. None of these problems was very severe; yet, they had been compounded by his parents' divorce and his mother's alcoholism during his first years of school.

By the time Allen was in junior high, his mother had conquered her illness through Alcoholics Anonymous and he had been helped by Alanon (a discussion group for children of alcoholic parents). Allen presented a picture of a child whose problems were emotionally and academically based. Therefore, the diagnostician referred him to an experienced learning disabilities specialist who could develop a warm therapeutic relationship.

Allen responded very well to individual tutoring and overcame his lags fairly quickly. His tutor discovered, however, that his main problem was his complete disorganization. He could not keep track of his assignments. Regularly, he forgot to bring his books home, and when he did, he often lost them on the way. His notebooks were a disaster. His school life would have been total chaos if his mother had not been so helpful. Feeling guilty about her behavior during her past illness, she tried especially hard to make up for it. She had faith in Allen and persisted in her belief that he could straighten out. She quickly assented when it was suggested that Allen attend a special school for children with emotional as well as learning problems. There he received psychotherapy. Several years later the boy was able to return to his own high school. Being able to cope with the work, he eventually graduated. Although work was never easy for Allen, he was able to go on to junior college.

Special Needs of the Older Learning-disabled Student

The learning-disabled adolescent at home

The learning-disabled adolescent needs guidance. Sometimes he responds well to parents; often he prefers taking advice from teachers or counselors. Parents must use their judgment. Most of the time parents can be of assistance at home by

1. Helping a student make a daily study schedule.
2. Finding a suitable place for him to study where distractions can be minimized.
3. Seeing that he uses an assignment notebook.
4. Checking that he keeps his course notebooks organized and up to date. If not, give him some assistance.
5. Knowing course requirements; checking that his work is done on time.
6. Helping him plan ahead for future assignments.
7. Replacing classroom texts with books containing similar material written on a lower level.
8. Obtaining textbooks in recorded form for the blind and for the print-handicapped from Recordings for the Blind, Inc., 215 East 58th St., New York, N.Y. 10022, which will save him from reading long assignments. Recorded textbooks are available on many subjects.
9. Discussing the necessity of untimed tests with their son or daughter and his or her counselor. Parents should be aware that, if necessary, the learning-disabled adolescent is permitted to take untimed P.S.A.T.'s and S.A.T.'s. They should be certain that the school has made arrangements for this through the Admissions Testing Program, Box 592-A, Princeton, N.J. 08541.

Learning-disabled adolescents
in the regular classroom

Many of the needs of the learning-disabled adolescent can be met within the regular classroom by making minor program modifications, such as the following:[3]

1. Scheduling the student into courses where he or she has the most likelihood of success, based on his or her learning style.
2. Presenting material in smaller sequential steps.
3. Reinforcing basic concepts with supplementary materials.
4. Arranging seating to minimize distractions.
5. Providing a course syllabus to overcome problems of disorganization.
6. Furnishing written records of homework assignments.
7. Providing a written copy of work put on the board to reduce copying errors and excessive time required by this task.
8. Permitting tape recording of lectures to allow the student to keep pace with the class.
9. Segmenting learning experiences into shorter time blocks to accommodate the student's short attention span.
10. Utilizing prerecorded textbooks in lieu of reading assignments.
11. Arranging for the student to take tests orally rather than in written form.
12. Removing time restrictions from tests, or administering tests in two sessions.
13. Substituting oral reports, graphic displays or other projects for written reports.
14. Replacing selected reading assignments with audio-visual presentations.
15. Contracting with the student for a grade based on fulfilling mutually agreed-upon course requirements.
16. Arranging for peer tutoring.
17. Providing positive feedback consistently and frequently.
18. Recognizing and utilizing special talents or areas of strength to promote learning.
19. Allowing the student to monitor his daily progress through the use of charts or graphs.
20. Communicating frequently with the LD resource teacher regarding the student's progress.
21. Reducing the learning-disabled student's load to four or even three credits per year, and scheduling a study hall in addition to LD resource services. (The learning-disabled student is eligible for ser-

[3]Gray, A.S., and D.K. Shriver, *A Secondary LD Resource Program Handbook for Teachers* (Augusta County, Va., Schools: 1978).

vices until age 21 if necessary to complete high school; for some students this may be a viable alternative.)

The learning-disabled
student in college

1. The above modifications are applicable to college as well as high school.
2. Because the workload at college may be very time-consuming, the learning-disabled student must be especially careful about signing up for too many extracurricular activities or participating in too many social functions.
3. In choosing a college, it is very important for the learning-disabled student to select one that understands the nature of learning disabilities and offers help and guidance when needed. Even more important is finding a college that has courses in which he can develop his strengths and interests, such as art, music, ceramics, computer science, marine biology, and so on. Many schools have college information centers and guidance counselors who are knowledgeable about all types of colleges. There are also private agencies and counselors in this field. Sometimes it is difficult to find the right college for the learning-disabled student; so start searching early. The Association for Children with Learning Disabilities, 4156 Library Road, Pittsburgh, Pa. 15234, provides a list of colleges and universities that accept students with learning disabilities.

The following are the thoughts of Ginny, a young adult, who had severe learning disabilities throughout her school years. She received intensive remedial help and eventually went to college. After graduation, Ginny found a successful career.

As I was growing up, I knew I had learning problems. What they were exactly I do not remember. I just remember that I had trouble reading and sounding out words, in writing paragraphs in order so they would make sense. In high school English class I remember I had trouble speaking and in keeping my words in order. I think that was from nerves and being afraid of making a mistake, as well as an inability to organize my thoughts.

Through all this, I had my parents behind me. They took me for extra help for a long time. My tutor and I became good friends but sometimes I would get frustrated because of all the extra work. My mother helped me with school projects. I used to have good ideas and get them all mixed up. We learned to work together.

I had trouble throughout my days going to suburban schools with high standards. I did do well in science because I was very interested in it and wanted to gain more knowledge. I think I would have done better in every subject, but everyone in all my classes was so competitive, which did not help a frustrated, nervous student like me. I just

*went on and did my best. Some of my teachers did not understand my
problems but some did and helped me with my subjects. When it came
to memorization I was tops. I can remember a lot of things. (This
helped too.)*

*At the suggestion of my guidance counselor I went on to a junior
college and did just fine. When I transferred, I finally ended up at a
four year college where I got my degree as a medical secretary. I
really had no trouble at all at the regular college. I received a lot of
praise which I never got from my high school teachers.*

*When I finally got my degree, of course, my uncertainties were about
where or when I would get a job. I got one right away and I enjoy
what I do.*

*Things really turned out well for me. Because my parents were
behind me and never pushed me, I never gave up hope about my
problems.*

*Every child has some special thing that she or he is interested in and
can do well. It is important to encourage this. Academic achievement
does not have to be stressed all the time.*

GINNY BAYER

FOR ADOLESCENTS AND ADULTS
WITH SEVERE PROBLEMS
IN READING AND ENGLISH

English That We Need, Helen Prevo, Frank E. Richards Publishing
Co., Inc., Phoenix, N.Y. 13135.

Getting It Down in Writing, Pal Practical Living Series, Xerox Education Publications, Columbus, Ohio 43216.

Life Skills Reading 1, by Carol Mullins, Educational Design, Inc., 47
W. 13th St., New York, N.Y. 10011.

Life Skills Reading 2, Comprehension Skills, by Carol Mullins, Educational Design, Inc., New York, N.Y. 10011.

Meeting Basic Competencies in Reading, by Dr. Eileen L. Corcoran,
Frank E. Richards Publishing Co., Inc., Phoenix, N.Y. 13135.

More English That We Need, Helen Prevo, Frank E. Publishing Co.,
Inc., Phoenix, N.Y. 13135.

Reading For Survival, Eileen L. Corcoran, Frank E. Richards Publishing Co., Inc., Phoenix, N.Y. 13135.

Scoring High in Survival Reading: Getting Around, Alvin Kravitz
and Dan Dramer, Random House, Inc., New York, N.Y.

Turner-Livingston Series, Follett Publishing Co., Chicago, Ill.: *The
Town You Live In, The Jobs You Get, The Person You Are, The Friends You
Make, The Television You Watch, The Phone Calls You Make, The News-
paper You Read, The Language You Speak.*

11 FACTORS INFLUENCING LEARNING, COPING WITH PROBLEMS

From childhood to adulthood it is necessary to acquire skills for academic learning. While we have focused on how children learn, in this chapter we want to highlight specific factors that influence learning—the child's intelligence; physical and neurological development; the attitudes of parents, families, and teachers; cultural and economic background; social and emotional behavior; and personality traits. All these aspects are an integral part of living as well as learning.

FACTORS INFLUENCING LEARNING

Lucy, who inherited her great-grandfather's mathematical ability, her mother's skill in writing, and her father's excellent sense of organization, was a lucky girl. Learning was much easier for her than for Kitty, whose genes were so shuffled that she took after her "not-so-bright" Aunt Mamie, and her father who had learning disabilities. Superior native ability is a wonderful gift. Yet, it must be realized that native ability may be stunted by illness, accident, undernourishment, deprivation, or trauma, all of which will also affect physical and neurological development.

Physical and neurological development depends on the maturation of the central nervous system, a complicated connective system between the body and the brain. Like maturation in other areas, it develops in sequential stages. However, brain injury and malfunctioning slow down the development of the central nervous system. As we have pointed out, there is a great variation in the development of children, but generally the age of

179

a child determines his physical, neurological and mental growth.

It is obvious that physical defects in hearing, vision, and speech retard learning, and should be checked very carefully in the early years. For example, Terry, who was an intelligent learning-disabled child with visual-spatial difficulties, had serious problems in reading and math. In addition, he was scared to ski and afraid to play baseball. At bat, he was afraid that he would be hit by the ball and worried that he could not connect. His eyes had been checked by the school nurse who stated that he he had 20–20 vision. However, his teacher reported that he could not copy from the blackboard, and continually lost his line in reading. The tutor discovered that Terry simply could not see likenesses and differences in designs, even after remedial instruction had been geared to his problems. At that point she surmised that his eyes must be the cause of the problem. The simplest pegboard designs were beyond him. Referred to the New York Eye and Ear Infirmary, which had a special department for orthoptics, Terry was given a thorough eye examination. This disclosed that he had muscular weakness and problems in fusion.

Initially he was given exercises at the infirmary. Then these exercises were continued with his mother, who had been trained by the therapist at the clinic. After a year Terry's eyes were operating normally and his improvement in visual-spatial relations was rapid. At that point, he started to respond to the required remediation in math and reading. After three years of tutoring, Terry was in the top half of his class and was admitted to a private school with high standards. There he was on the honor roll. Nevertheless, Terry still reads slowly and most likely always will. Another result of improved vision was a complete turnaround in his attitude towards sports. Now, he is an enthusiastic skier, a good golfer, and an excellent tennis player.

In our experience, the attitudes of parents and teachers profoundly affect a child's learning. Parents' continual faith and encouragement make a child feel better about himself and motivate him to learn. In Terry's case, his progress was enhanced by his parents' attitudes. His mother and father were caring and supportive. In particular, over a long period of time his mother was conscientious in helping Terry with his work and attending to his eye exercises and checkups. Above all, his mother and father accepted his problems and did not pressure him. Many parents are equally conscientious with their children. However, there are times when one parent feels that the other is fostering dependence by being overprotective, and there is disagreement between the mother and father. Wise parents realize that sometimes a child needs a little more shove, and at other times, a little more indulgence.

All parents dream and hope that their children will do well in life. They want to help them as much as possible. Children expect their mothers and fathers to show interest in their school work and activities. On the other hand, if there is too much concern about their studies and pursuits, children will worry about their performance. They want to please their parents and they may equate their successes and failures with gaining or losing approval and love. Parents can bring pressure in different ways: some fret constantly about report cards; others plague their children about daily achievements; still others insist on their children attending schools whose standards are beyond their capacities, and urge their consideration of colleges which are out of reach.

Herbert was pressured in this way. After a number of years, he overcame his learning disabilities to the extent that he could cope in a regular classroom. At the end of elementary school, his father, an outstanding business executive, contrary to professional advice, persisted in sending Herbert to a difficult prep school. Of course, the results were disastrous. Herbert's father really cared for his son but, like many extremely successful people, he felt that his judgment was good in all matters. When mothers and fathers are too ambitious, their demands and pressures may lead to frustration and apprehension. In turn these feelings lower self-esteem and interfere with learning.

Teachers who give children confidence and show high expectations for their ability tend to generate success in their students. Conversely, teachers who make their pupils feel less than adequate because of low expectations stifle school achievement. Excessively demanding teachers affect children the same way overly demanding parents do.

As we have emphasized throughout this book, teaching should be geared to the developmental level of the youngsters, and expectations should not be greater than their capacity. Teachers must be aware when the curriculum is too difficult for some of their students. If they make unrealistic demands, children will develop more problems, such as anxiety, regression, dislike of school, and sometimes school phobia. Continuing unrealistic demands in the upper grades may provoke students to become truants or school dropouts.

Children's cultural and economic background also influences their learning. There is a wide variation of cultures in our country, and attitudes toward learning differ. If a child comes from a deprived background he is usually handicapped when he enters our schools. Depending on the geographical area in which he lives, he sometimes does not know our language, and even if he does, he has probably missed early language and intellectual stimulation. Generally his parents are too poverty-stricken, harried, or uneducated to give him meaningful experiences which help develop concepts. Education in our American schools is primarily geared to the middle class, and a disadvantaged child usually lacks preparation for coping in kindergarten and first grade.

Fortunately, disadvantaged children can be helped by preschool programs designed to develop the social, language, and basic readiness skills not fostered in their home environment. The need for this type of program was recognized early in the 1960s. Dr. Martin Deutsch, a psychologist who was the Director of the Institute for Developmental Studies in New York, was a leader in the movement. He designed experimental programs to prepare poor and deprived youngsters for school. Other programs were also initiated during the 1960s by Omar Khayyam Moore, who developed the talking typewriter, Carl Bereiter and Siegfried Engelmann, who developed the Distar program, and disciples of Maria Montessori, who incorporated her methods and materials in preschool programs for disadvantaged children. One of the best-known projects was Head Start, part of President Johnson's Great Society legislation.

Head Start was a laboratory for many future programs that multiplied all over the United States. Their effectiveness was debated, but recent research studies have proved that preschool education can be beneficial. Several studies[1] have shown that preschool education for the disadvantaged can prevent school failure and can result in better academic performance, less need for remedial programs, less delinquency, and a more positive outlook for employment.

New programs concentrate on child rearing at the infant level. Some projects involve training parents within the home environment, teaching parents how to communicate with their babies, and how to develop babies' interest in the world around them. In addition, preventive psychiatry is reaching down to the preschool child. The Center for Preventive Psychiatry in White Plains, N.Y., is a pioneer in this field.

While preschool education is vital for the disadvantaged child, it can be important for other children. Nursery schools, child care centers, and playgroups give them the opportunity to develop emotionally and socially. For obvious reasons, learning-disabled children, who are often slow to mature, gain from good preschool education. Their parents also profit from observing their boys and girls with other children and learn from the counseling of knowledgeable nursery school teachers. If the child is slow to mature, remaining in nursery school an extra year is advisable. For the immature child who does not attend nursery school, repeating kindergarten is better than being kept back in first grade.

Immature social behavior will seriously affect a child's learning no matter how bright he is. If he is unable to sit still, concentrate, or pay attention, he cannot learn.

Children with specific learning disabilities vary greatly in their behavior patterns. Many with minor learning disabilities are quiet and controlled; these are the children who are not pressured by their parents and who understand and accept their own problems. These youngsters are usually well-adjusted, work hard, and are liked by their classmates. By contrast, the behavior of many learning-disabled youngsters may be very

[1]High/Scope Educational Research Foundation Study, Ypsilanti, Michigan, conducted by Lawrence J. Schweinhart and David R. Weikart. Study by Dr. Irving Lazar and team, Consortium on Developmental Continuity, based at Cornell University, Ithaca, N.Y.

trying at home and in school; they tend to be distractible, completely disorganized, and impulsive.

Surprisingly enough, these same children may become so absorbed in a task or activity that they continue doing the same thing over and over again in a robotlike way. In talking they seem to get stuck on one subject and often sound like a broken record. This continued repetition or protracted activity, which they seem powerless to stop on their own, is called perseveration. This trait spills over to all types of school learning. For example, in handwriting, the child writes the *n* like an *m* or *mm*. In math, the child gives the same answer to different problems. In reading, she adds endings to words—*hurried* becomes *hurrieded*. Furthermore, perseveration hinders the child from changing from one process to another—switching from addition to subtraction. This tendency makes her rigid and inflexible when it comes to adopting new routines and accepting changes in plans.

Nate is an example of an impulsive, perseverating child, who is continually in motion. In the classroom, he constantly pops up to sharpen one pencil after another. While in orbit, he tries to distract the class with funny faces and amusing gestures. Like many learning-disabled children, Nate is clowning to cover up his feelings of inadequacy and depression and to gain attention from his classmates. Hilary, another learning-disabled child, also has feelings of inadequacy and depression, but she is not hyperactive. On the contrary she withdraws and sits docilely in her chair daydreaming, letting her mind wander far afield. Hilary seeks to escape from a world of fears and failures. Some of the other ways that children cope with frustration are: blaming others for their troubles, complaining of aches and pains (only on school days), returning to infantile behavior, and covering up their anger by being passive.

Because the learning-disabled boy or girl is inclined to be impulsive, he or she rarely takes time to reflect upon or analyze a given task. This type of youngster simply does or says the first thing that pops into his or her mind. Teachers and parents can help. He or she must be slowed down and reminded to think before acting or talking. When the teacher recommended to Leslie that she count to ten before responding to a question, she surprised everyone by being correct most of the time. Another youngster must be shown strategies—how to analyze and tackle a particular task. Billy was able to handle his science project on snakes when his teacher called him up after class and discussed the following suggestions: write about four different kinds of snakes—find out what they look like, where they live, what their habits are, what they eat, and how they protect themselves. This planful approach gave him the direction he needed.

Specific approaches to helping the impulsive, hyperactive child include the use of medication, diet, and behavior modification. In our experience, we found short term medication has been miraculous for some but completely ineffective with others. On occasion, drowsiness is a side effect. As with all medicine, the right dosage and proper administration is critical. The subject of special diets is controversial. However, we have seen some children who were practically climbing the walls quiet down when all sweets, particularly chocolate, were eliminated from their diet.

The use of behavior modification has been frequently effective in developing and sustaining appropriate behavior. It focuses on positive reinforcement accompanied by tangible rewards and praise. For example, a teacher makes a contract with Johnny, who talks out loud constantly. She will offer him a gumdrop if he is quiet for a specified amount of time (say 10 minutes). Gradually, he must be quiet for longer periods of time in order to receive a gumdrop. All Johnny's successes will be rewarded by social praise—a smile, a pat on the back—as well as a gumdrop. Finally it is hoped that he will be reasonably quiet without any tangible rewards. There is certainly nothing new about motivating good behavior through rewards, and behavior modification is based on a reward system. However, behavior modification is a highly structured procedure which requires much planning and thought to administer successfully.

Most children seem to settle down at some point, but the learning-disabled hyperkinetic child is slow to do so. In the meantime, he has not been learning. However, at around the age of nine or ten he usually becomes less active. Most doctors and experienced professionals feel that the combination of appropriate educational techniques and sensible management by parents and school is the best approach. Equally important is the teacher's understanding of how a child learns and how he or she can be motivated.

It must be understood that children with primary emotional problems exhibit many of the same behavioral disorders typical of the learning-disabled child: distractibility, poor impulse control, weak retention abilities, poor concentration. If problems are emotionally based, the first priority should be psychotherapy for the child and the family. A child has to be receptive to learning before he can be taught. Most of the time, therapy opens the door. Because of the similarity of symptoms in the learning-disabled and the emotionally disturbed, psychiatrists often require a psycho-educational evaluation that will help determine the primary cause.

A parent should be conscious of the types of tests that make up an evaluation, and the results of the testing should be explained to them in nontechnical language in terms of the child's strengths and weaknesses. Parents should be able to communicate freely with the school psychologist or the specialist who administers the test. In turn, a child should be prepared for a testing situation. He should be told in simple clear terms why he is being tested: to discover his capabilities, to choose the correct school program, to help him do better work and so on.

In most cases, emotional problems of the learning-disabled children are the result of frustration from their learning disabilities. A child's family his parents, grandparents, brothers, and sisters, can all contribute to his success or failure. If he is to overcome or compensate for his problems, he needs family support.

Unfortunately, some learning-disabled children, because of their personality traits, may present difficult and trying situations at home and in school. They may pick fights with their siblings and classmates, fatigue easily, and explode unpredictably. It is not difficult to understand that these children also may have immature social perception. They continue too long to be egocentric and do not understand other people's intentions. Their inability to focus, pay attention, and discriminate visual and auditory signals contribute to poor social adjustment. They may not distinguish facial expressions such as approval and disapproval, realize that a raised voice denotes anger, or sense when their classmates are annoyed by their actions or words. They are inclined to say or do the wrong thing at the wrong time. Consequently, they often have trouble forming friendships and are lonely. This rejection worries them, and their unhappy social situation interferes with their learning. These children need to be taught step-by-step socialization skills as well as academic skills. Problems of social adjustment may extend until adolescence or young adulthood, at which time they require particular attention and continued instruction.

Teachers and parents must recognize that children differ widely in their temperaments and personality traits. Mrs. Stanley's four children had distinct personalities of their own. The oldest, Amy, was happy and bouncy. Every new experience was a joy and if something went wrong, her tears subsided quickly. The second, Lee, was the vulnerable one; if someone looked at him critically, he dissolved into tears. Every mishap was a tragedy; he was shy and adjusted slowly to new situations. Janet, the third, was the hard-working student of the family. Although she did not have Lee's high I.Q., she brought home better report cards; she had a drive to achieve. The youngest, Ronny, could have joined the Marines at the age of ten; he was the tough guy of the family; at times only stern discipline would impress him. Just as Mrs. Stanley had to learn to handle each child differently, so did their teachers. Not only must parents and teachers deal with the overly active youngsters, but they also must motivate and give support to the shy, withdrawn children.

Stella Chess, in *Temperament and Learning Ability of School Children*, states that "For the slow-to-warm-up child or the difficult child, initial school experiences can be crucial. They can give him the firm conviction that school is a frightening and traumatic situation, which confronts him with kaleidoscopic demands that are impossible for him to meet. This negative experience may be modified if the child is given an opportunity to adapt slowly while a minimum number of changes and new demands are introduced. He may learn that although he is bewildered or made to feel strange by a new situation, he eventually not only masters it but gains a great deal of pleasure from it. With the negative interaction, however, the child can develop anxiety."[2] Dr. Chess emphasizes the "significance of . . . a child's temperamental organization" in learning.[3]

WHAT TO DO ABOUT
LEARNING PROBLEMS

Both children and adults need assistance when they have learning problems. While skills taught and remedial techniques used may be similar, materials will usually differ. Attitudes generally differ too: the adult is more self-motivated, self-directed, and realistic about his strengths and weaknesses.

In helping a child, it is important to remember that he or she has intense feelings even at a very young age and can feel depressed, anxious, and mortified. A parent or teacher is more sensitive to a pupil's feelings if he or she can remember his or her own childhood. He should try to recall a day when everyone laughed and giggled and he felt humiliated because he gave a stupid answer in class. Perhaps this only happened occasionally. He should think of the children for whom this is a daily experience; they are afraid to open their mouths.

Some Types of Youngsters
Who Need Help

1. Children who are just a little below grade level because of having "horsed around," as they put it, or because of illness and long absences. They lap up instruction. They are eager to learn and fun to teach.

2. Youngsters who are unresponsive, passive, and afraid to try. They have to learn to express their feelings. A little success and encouragement will give them a boost.

3. Those who are hostile and aggressive. In a class, they are the behavior problems, but in a one-to-one situation, they can be cooperative. Although they are angry and frustrated, they really want to succeed. They respond to individual attention.

4. Those who are anxious and frightened and rush at everything impulsively. They want to please, but cannot dig for their own resources. Having little inner strength, they have very poor images of themselves; they need support. These children respond to what we call the "Walter Mitty" treatment: have them pretend—act out the role of the strong man in the circus, a queen sitting on the throne, or Babe Ruth at bat.

[2]Stella Chess, M.D., "Temperament and Learning Ability of School Children," *American Journal of Public Health*, vol. 58, No. 12 (December, 1968), 2237–38.

[3]Chess, "Temperament and Learning Ability of School Children," 2239.

Children often understand their problems better when they read about fictional characters and real people who have similar problems. (Use of books for this purpose is called bibliotherapy.)[4] In identifying with people who have overcome adversity, children become more hopeful and learn to cope with their own stressful situations. Moreover, books that deal with a particular child's problem can be a starting point for discussion between the child and an adult. Sharing reactions to painful life experiences portrayed in books encourages a child to express his feelings. A child often has fears and fantasies which can be dispelled by an understanding adult.

By observing different children react to failure one can also gain insight about their inner feelings. Some respond by acting silly, others by anger, some by sadness and defeat, and others by yawning. There is a common denominator in the educational approach. We know that learning will not take place until undesirable attitudes are changed. There is no level too low to begin teaching and one can always find a level where a child succeeds. Once he has gained confidence through successful experiences, he can gradually be given more difficult material so he can learn to cope with harder tasks. A child has to be capable of tolerating some frustration, making an effort, and using his own resources—otherwise he will never be able to function in the classroom, on the playground, or in or outside of his home.

There is no blueprint on how to help a child meet frustration—when and how one does this. Instincts have to be the guide.

Volunteers who have *never* taught, or who have not taught for years, may be concerned about their own capabilities. Parents and grandparents especially should not doubt their qualifications. They have all been teachers since the birth of their first child. Mothers are children's first teachers, for better or for worse. They have lived with children, day in and day out, year in and year out. They know what makes them tick. With this natural endowment, they have had experience that can carry over to teaching. Parents, grandparents, and people who have had contact with children, or people from large families, can learn the techniques, tools, and some of the knowledge provided to teachers in training; think what an enriched teaching potential they have. They should not sell themselves short.

Approaches to Use
When Working Individually

1. Find out as much as possible about the child.

2. Get acquainted; build rapport:

     Give him a puzzle, joke book, or game to relax him.

---

[4]A list of books dealing with physical and mental handicaps, learning disabilities, and emotional problems involving young people follows this chapter.

State good things you have heard about him—for example, he's the best soccer player or the best artist in the class.

Tell him why you are there—to help him improve.

Ask the child to talk about himself—listen to his language; find out his interests—favorite TV shows, books, sports, music; ask him to describe his family; how he feels about school.

Tell him that he is not stupid, that everyone has some problems. Tell him about yours: for example, reversal of telephone numbers, difficulty following directions to unfamiliar places, and so on.

Give him a chance to ventilate his feelings.

3. Teaching:

On the basis of his or her needs, plan teaching with creative and school materials—make the lessons interesting and fun.

Always structure lessons with appropriate timing and different activities. A child is interested in the agenda; end with a "treat" (a game or story). Later on, he or she may be able to plan the lesson with you.

Vary techniques: a duller child may be more satisfied with routine techniques; a brighter child generally needs more diversification.

Many classroom skills can be taught through activities in gym, music, and art. Use these special subjects to help a child learn basic abilities—for example, math through music, gym, and shop; spatial relations through art and gym; following directions in all activities; and so on.

It must always be remembered that education is not confined to the classroom. Think of the opportunities at camp—in arts and crafts, nature study, swimming, sports; at home—in cooking, gardening, painting, sewing.

Use experiences from one's own background to extend the child's knowledge and interest in the world around him.

Parents of learning-disabled children at one time were at the mercy of professionals: a pediatrician who informed them that there was nothing wrong with their child, a principal who insisted that their child was not intelligent, a psychologist who considered his problems entirely emotional. But not anymore. Most people now understand learning disabilities. Much of the advancement in the area of specific learning disabilities has come from the work of parent and professional organizations. One of the first was the Orton Society, Inc., named for Samuel T. Orton, a neurologist and a pioneer in the field of specific language disabilities (dyslexia). The Society provides leadership in the study of language problems, research, and publications, all related to dyslexia. It also offers resources for evaluation and remediation throughout the country. Its membership includes teachers, doctors, psychologists, and parents.

Over the years, local parental groups interested in learning disabilities have sprung up all over the country. These organizations have alerted schools to learning disabilities, and pressured them to modify school programs for those youngsters who were not able to cope with regular school work. As time went on these local groups banded together with professionals and formed organizations, such as the Association for Children with Learning Disabilities (ACLD), which has fifty state chapters and many local chapters. Parents can write to the ACLD main headquarters, 2200 Brownsville Rd., Pittsburgh, Pa. 15210. When requested, it will refer parents to the nearest local chapter, where they can get assistance in finding appropriate help for diagnosis and remediation.

The ACLD also provides information on pending legislation on learning disabilities. It was active in the passage of PL94-142, Education Act for ALL Handicapped Children, in 1975. This bill mandates a free appropriate education for all handicapped children and includes specific learning disabilities as a handicapping condition. It states that handicapped children must be educated in the "least restrictive environment," which means children should be mainstreamed in the public schools as much as possible. The Education Act also requires that a written individualized educational program be developed at least annually for the children affected and that it should indicate their present level of functioning, the special services which will be provided, and annual goals. While the goals of this legislation are admirable, the program demands more funding in order to help all those who need it. Parents must investigate to see if their child is eligible for this program and if so they should realize that they are legally included in the decision-making. One must always bear in mind that the continuation of these services depends on congressional appropriations and that these services can be limited or discontinued by budget cuts and new legislation. It is important to keep abreast of the changes in state and federal legislation. In addition to contacting the ACLD for legislative information, there is a toll-free number for people seeking information on Federal legislation and issues relating to the handicapped. (MAINSTREAM-ON-CALL: 1-800-424-8089, weekdays)

Because of budgetary limitations, numerous schools cannot provide the type of individual help they would like to offer the learning-disabled. Throughout the country many schools have turned to volunteers. The more funds are cut, the more need there is for volunteers. In our experience, volunteers who are well trained and under supervision have made a significant contribution toward helping the learning-disabled.

In some situations, parents may seek private help. If they do, they should be aware that a number of major medical insurance policies cover services for evaluations, tutoring, and psychiatric help. Parents should also be aware that the cost of educating a child with learning disabilities may be considered a tax-deductible medical expense. If the child meets the requirements (to be determined by a physician), his parents may be able to deduct the cost of diagnostic evaluation, special education groups, tutoring, transportation and materials.

HELP FOR THE ADULT

More and more adults are becoming aware of the root of their learning problems, and are seeking help. While tutors remediate their weaknesses, they must also show these adults how to use their strengths. This was done with Tom, whose main difficulties were poor written expression and disorganization. Tom spoke easily and fluently and had an outgoing personality. For a time he could talk convincingly, but after a while he would begin to ramble on and on in a diffuse way. Part of his tutoring included preparation for sales talks and oral business reports. He was taught to outline his thoughts briefly so he would keep on the track. In order to improve his ability to dictate, he learned to list his points and to express them orally. Since he was so fluent, he quickly became proficient at dictation. Once he learned not to be so verbose, he could work very well with customers.

We want to suggest to adults with learning disabilities that they focus on their strengths, whether they lie in math, science, speaking, writing, art, music or a particular sport; or in an attractive personality, pleasant telephone voice, or thoroughness.

In the past it was the learning-disabled child who received attention. Recently, a number of organizations have been formed to serve adolescents and adults with learning disabilities. Through these organizations, learning-disabled adults meet other learning-disabled adults for the first time; they discover they are not alone, and that many others are facing similar difficulties. They share the same concerns: finding and holding jobs, securing an accurate diagnosis of their strengths and weaknesses, locating appropriate help for overcoming learning problems, obtaining legal information, taking untimed tests for college or civil service. The President's Committee on the Employment of the Handicapped has written a comprehensive pamphlet entitled *Learning Disabilities: Not Just a Problem Children Outgrow:* The President's Committee on the Employment of the Handicapped, Washington, D.C. 20210. For the learning-disabled adult, it describes many nationwide groups and the services they provide. Organizations for the learning-disabled—child, adolescent, and adult—are listed at the end of this chapter.

While building rapport and encouraging self-confidence is basic to all teaching, the primary goal is to raise the individual's level of academic functioning by giving him the appropriate tools for learning. Once a student has acquired some skills, he or she will encounter successful learning experiences, which in turn will generate self-confidence and a greater desire to learn. Raising an individual's self-esteem and level of achievement is educational therapy, which leads to better learning.

RESOURCES AVAILABLE FOR CHILDREN, ADOLESCENTS, AND ADULTS

Association for Children with Learning Disabilities, 2200 Brownsville Road, Pittsburgh, Pa. 15210. The headquarters is in Pittsburgh, and local branches exist throughout the country.

ACLD, Association for Children and Adults with Learning Disabilities, 4156 Library Road, Pittsburgh, Pa., 15234 (412-231-7977) *Youth and Adult Section.* Compiles a list of college programs which make allowances for learning disabilities. Cost $1.00.

AFL-CIO Human Resource Development Institute (HRD). Contact Handicapped Coordinator, 815 16th St. NW, Washington, D.C. 20006 (202-638-3914). Helps handicapped people find jobs.

Closer Look, Box 1492, Washington, D.C. 20013 (202-833-4160). Gives information on employment rights, higher education, and groups concerned with disabled people.

Foundation for Children with Learning Disabilities, 99 Park Avenue, New York, N.Y. 10017. The headquarters is in New York, and local branches exist throughout the country.

National Library Service for the Blind and Physically Handicapped. The Library of Congress, Washington, D.C. 20542 (202-882-5500). Supplies free recorded books and equipment. To be eligible for their services, applicant must be certified by a doctor as having a "reading disability" due to organic dysfunctions.

The Orton Dyslexic Society, 8415 Bellona Lane, Towson, Md. 21204. Local branches exist throughout the country.

Partners in Publishing (PIP) sells a newsletter, a directory of college programs for learning-disabled students, and a handbook of aids for the college bound.

Recordings for the Blind, Inc., 215 E. 58 St., New York, N.Y. 10022. Tapes textbooks at the request of blind or print-handicapped students. To use services, students must be certified by a qualified person such as a doctor, therapist, or counselor.

ALDA—Association of Learning Disabled Adults, P.O. Box 9722, Friendship Station, Washington, D.C. 20016—a group started and run by learning-disabled adults, with regular open meetings, at which adults discuss how they cope with their difficulties.

TOTE Time Out to Enjoy, Chicago, Ill.

BIBLIOTHERAPY LIST

Guides

Bernstein, Lois. *Books to Help Children Cope with Separation and Loss*. New York and London: R. R. Bowker, 1977.

Fassler, Joan. *Helping Children Cope, Mastering Stress through Books and Stories*. New York: The Free Press, a division of Macmillan Publishers, 1978.

Fiction

Albert, Louise. *But I'm Ready to Go* (1976). Feeling rejected, unimportant and alienated from her family, 15-year-old Judy devises a secret plan to make people admire her.

Blue, Rose. *Me and Einstein* (1979). Having tried for years to hide the fact that he can't read, a nine-year-old boy finally discovers the reason for his problem.

Brancato, Robin. *Winning* (1977). Paralyzed in a football accident, high school student Gary struggles to accept and overcome his condition, with the dedicated assistance of recently widowed English teacher Ann Treer.

Brown, Roy. *Find Debbie* (1976). A detective's objectivity mixes with his emotions during his search for Debbie, a retarded child who is reported missing, but not particularly missed, by her parents and siblings.

Byars, Betsy. *The Summer of the Swans* (1970). A warm, humorous story of a young person at odds with her self and the world during a difficult fourteenth summer.

Cleaver, Vera. *Me Too* (1973). Lydia embarks on a stubborn campaign to help her retarded twin sister and learns an important lesson in the process.

Corcoran, Barbara. *Axe-Time, Sword-Time* (1976). On the eve of World War II, a young girl handicapped by a reading disability tries to cope with family problems and the question of her future.

Cross, Helen Reeder. *The Real Tom Thumb* (1980). The story of a boy who never grew taller than 31 inches, yet became a world celebrity.

De Angeli, Margarite. *The Door in the Wall* (1949). A crippled boy wanted to be a knight, but kindly monks find another way for him to serve the king.

Golo, Phyllis. *Please Don't Say Hello* (1975). A family with an autistic son named Eddie moves into a new house and explains to the neighborhood children how they and the special school Eddie attends can help the boy.

Green, Hannah. *I Never Promised You a Rose Garden* (1964). A realistic account of a teen-age girl's struggle to overcome the self-destruction of her schizophrenia.

Grohskopf, Bernice. *Shadow in the Sun* (1975). Arriving in Cape Cod for the summer, Fran accepts a position as companion to a crippled girl of her own age.

Guest, Judith. *Ordinary People* (1976). Seventeen-year-old Conrad returns to his home and tries to build a new life for himself after spending 8 months in a mental institution for attempted suicide.

Levoy, Myron. *Alan and Naomi* (1977). Alan avoids the crazy-acting French girl who has just moved into his building in New York until he learns that she has recently seen her father killed by the Gestapo in Paris.

Keeton, Elizabeth B. *Emeralda* (1976). Emeralda's school year gets off to a bad start! She is still the smallest girl in the class and the town girls are snooty. With humor and understanding, the author shows how Emeralda learns to cope and grow up.

Keith, Harold. *The Runt of Rogers School* (1971). A small boy learns that spunk and ingenuity often mean more than size.

Killilea, Marie. *Karen* (1952). This is the story of a courageous girl who has cerebral palsy and the loving support she receives from her entire family.

Le Shan, Eda. *What Makes Me Feel This Way? Growing up with Human Emotions.* The book explains the importance of feelings, even those that confuse and frighten. Excellent for parents as well as children.

Little, Jean. *Take Wing* (1979). A moving story of a girl caught between her shyness and her strong determination to protect her handicapped brother.

Melton, David. *A Boy Called Hopeless* (1973). Fifteen-year-old Mary Jane describes her family's reactions when they discover that her younger brother is brain injured and their decision to participate in a program of rehabilitation together.

Muehl, Lois. *The Hidden Years of Devin Bates* (1967). Dev is an individual who rebels against being pushed to conform. He would prefer watching kids than joining school activities. Dev's father also pressures him about achievement.

Parker, Richard. *He Is Your Brother* (1974). Mike's reluctant attention to his withdrawn younger brother, Orry, and his sharing with Orry his interest in trains result in unanticipated adventure, respect, and growth for both boys.

Read, Elfrieda. *Brothers by Choice* (1974). The story of Rocky, an adopted older son who runs away from home. It is an exciting adventure story which probes the problems of adoption.

Rodowsky, Colby. *What About Me?* (1976). During an eventful year of heartbreak and difficult decisions, a talented high school girl gains insight into human emotions and her feelings about her mongoloid brother.

Sherburne, Zoe. *Why Have the Birds Stopped Singing?* (1974). An epileptic girl has a seizure that returns her in a journey of time to the period of her ancestors.

Slepian, Jan. *The Alfred Summer* (1980). A retarded boy and a boy with cerebral palsy become close friends and work on a project together. Their story shows that there are many ways of being "special."

Southall, Ivan. *Let the Balloon Go* (1968). A spastic child attempts a difficult feat that results in a fine achievement and greater understanding of himself.

Spence, Eleanor. *The Devil Hole* (1977). Feeling partly responsible for his brother Carl's strange, alienated, and disruptive behavior, Douglas is torn between loyalty to his family and his own interests and desires.

Spencer, Zane. *Cry of the Wolf* (1977). Feeling responsible for his father's death in a truck accident, sixteen-year-old Jim makes a slow recovery from his wounds until another crisis stirs him to action.

Stein, Sara Bonnett. *The Adopted One: An Open Family Book for Parents and Children Together* (1979). Vivid photographs and a simple honest text unfold the story for the child, while parents and teachers follow an accompanying text that provides more specific details.

Storr, Catherine. *Thursday* (1972). A fifteen-year-old girl attempts to help an emotionally confused boy accept life's realities.

Nonfiction

Axline, Virginia. *Dibs in Search of Self* (1964). The renowned, deeply moving story of an emotionally lost child who found his way back.

Brown, Marion Marsh. *The Silent Storm* (1963). The story of Annie Sullivan, the courageous teacher of Helen Keller.

Horwitz, Elinor. *Madness, Magic and Medicine* (1977). The treatment and mistreatment of the mentally ill.

Kaufman, Barry Neil. *Son-Rise* (1976). Against all professional advice and unknown odds, two parents record their autistic son's transformation from a lifeless, totally withdrawn child into an affectionate, loving and highly verbal little boy.

Langone, John. *Goodbye to Bedlam* (1974). Understanding mental illness and retardation.

MacCracken, Mary. *Lovey: A Very Special Child* (1976). Mary MacCracken records the ways in which she guided an emotionally disturbed eight-year-old on a long, difficult journey to reality and security.

Vallens, Evans. *A Long Way Up* (1966). The story of Jill Kinmont.

BIBLIOGRAPHY

Understanding Learning Problems
and Learning Disabilities

Chess, Stella, M.D., with Jane Whitbread, *How to Help Your Child Get the Most Out of School.* Garden City, N.Y.: Doubleday & Co., Inc., 1974.

Clark, Louise, *Can't Read, Can't Write, Can't Talk Too Good Either.* New York: Walker and Co., 1973.

Cohen, Dorothy H., *The Learning Child.* New York: Vintage Books, 1973.

Crosby, R.M.N., *The Waysiders.* New York: Delacorte Press, 1968.

Freiberg, Selma, *The Magic Years.* New York: Charles Scribner's Sons, 1959.

Gordon, Sol, *Living Fully: A Guide for Young People with a Handicap, Their Parents, Their Teachers and Professionals.* New York: The John Day Co., 1975.

Lynn, Roa with Neil D. Gluckin and Bernard Kripke, *Learning Disabilities: An Overview of Theories, Approaches, and Politics.* New York: The Free Press, Macmillan, Inc., 1979.

Kagan, J., and R. Cole, *Twelve to Sixteen—Early Adolescence.* New York: W.W. Norton & Co., Inc., 1972.

Lewis, Richard S., Alfred A. Strauss, and Laura E. Lehtinen, *The Other Child: The Brain-Injured Child.* New York: Grune & Stratton, Inc., 1961.

Natchez, Gladys, *Gideon.* New York: Basic Books, Inc., Publishers, 1975.

Osman, Betty B., *Learning Disabilities: A Family Affair.* New York: Random House, Inc., 1979.

Siegel, E., *The Exceptional Child Grows Up.* New York: E.P. Dutton, 1974.

Siegel, E., *Helping the Brain Injured Child.* New York: Association for Brain Injured Children, 1962.

Simpson, Eileen, *Reversals: A Personal Account of Victory Over Dyslexia.* Boston: Houghton-Mifflin Co., 1979.

Smith, Sally L., *No Easy Answers, The Learning Disabled Child.* Cambridge, Mass.: Winthrop Publishers, 1979.

Standing, E.M., *Maria Montessori: Her Life and Work.* New York: Mentor-Omega Books. New American Library of World Literature, Inc., 1968.

Stewart, M., and S. Olds, *Raising a Hyperactive Child.* New York: Harper & Row, Publishers, Inc., 1973.

Weber, Robert E. (Editor, N.J. Association for Children with Learning Disabilities) *Handbook on Learning Disabilities: A Prognosis for the Child, the Adolescent, the Adult.* Englewood Cliffs, N.J.: Prentice-Hall, Inc., 1974.

Teaching Children and Adults

FOR NEWCOMERS TO TUTORING OR TEACHING

Ames, Louise Bates, and Frances L. Ilg, *School Readiness.* New York: Harper & Row, Publishers, Inc., 1972.

Ashton-Warner, Sylvia, *Teacher.* New York: Simon and Schuster, Inc., 1963.

Developmental Language and Speech Center Staff, Grand Rapids, Michigan, *Teach Your Child to Talk.* New York: CEBCO/Standard Publishing Co., 1957.

Gesell, Arnold, M.D., and Frances L. Ilg, *The Child from Five to Ten.* New York: Harper & Row, Publishers, Inc., 1946.

Golick, M., *A Parent's Guide to Learning Problems.* Quebec Association for Children with Learning Disabilities, 6338 Victoria Avenue, Montreal 252, Quebec, Canada, 1970.

Heilman, Arthur W., *Phonics in Proper Perspective.* Columbus, Ohio: Charles E. Merrill Publishing Co., 1964.

Jenkins, Peggy Davison, *The Magic of Puppetry.* Englewood Cliffs, N.J.: Prentice-Hall, Inc., 1980.

Pines, Maya, *Revolution in Learning.* New York: Harper & Row, Publishers, Inc., 1962.

Pope, Lillie, *Guidelines to Teaching Remedial Reading.* Brooklyn, N.Y.: Faculty Press, 1975.

Sharp, Evelyn, *Thinking Is Child's Play.* New York: The Hearst Corporation, Avon Books, 1969.

Weiss, Martin S., and Helen Ginandes Weiss, *Home Is a Learning Place.* Boston: Little, Brown & Co., 1976.

Yahres, Herbert, *Learning Disabilities: Problems and Progress,* Public Affairs Committee, Inc., 381 Park Avenue South, New York, N.Y. 10016, 1979.

MORE ADVANCED BOOKS

Almy, Millie, with Edward Chittenden and Paula Miller, *Young Children's Thinking—Studies of Some Aspects of Piaget's Thinking.* New York: Teachers College Press, 1967.

Chall, Jean, *Learning to Read: The Great Debate.* New York: McGraw-Hill Book Company, 1967.

DeHirsch, K., and J. Jansky, *Predicting Reading Failure*. New York: Harper & Row, Publishers, Inc., 1965.

Durkin, Dolores, *Teaching Them to Read*. Boston: Allyn and Bacon, Inc., 1970.

Hamill, D.D., *Teaching Children with Learning and Behavior Problems*. Boston: Allyn & Bacon, Inc., 1975.

Harris, A.J., and E. Sipay, *How to Increase Reading Ability*. New York: David McKay Co., Inc., 1975.

Heilman, Arthur W., *Principles and Practices in Teaching Reading*. Columbus, Ohio: Charles E. Merrill Publishing Co., 1965.

Jansky, J., and K. DeHirsch, *Preventing Reading Failure*. New York: Harper & Row Publishers, Inc., 1972.

Johnson, D.J., and H.R. Mykelbust, *Learning Disabilities*. New York: Grune & Stratton, Inc., 1967.

Kephart, N.G., *The Slow Learner in the Classroom*. Columbus, Ohio: Charles E. Merrill Publishing Co., 1960.

Lerner, Janet, *Children with Learning Disabilities*. Boston: Houghton-Mifflin Co., 1971.

McCarthy, James J., and Joan F. McCarthy, *Learning Disabilities*. Boston: Allyn & Bacon, Inc., 1967.

Monroe, M., and B. Rogers, *Foundations for Reading*. Glenview, Ill.: Scott, Foresman & Co., 1964.

Ollilia, Lloyd O., *Handbook for Administrators and Teachers: Reading in the Kindergarten*. Newark, Delaware: International Reading Association (P.O. Box 8139, Newark, Delaware), 1980.

Riggs, Maida L., *Jump to Joy*. Englewood Cliffs, N.J.: Prentice-Hall, Inc., 1980.

Robinson, A., *Teaching Reading and Study Strategies: The Content Areas*. Boston: Allyn & Bacon, Inc., 1976.

Roswell, Florence, and Gladys Natchez, *Reading Disability, Diagnosis & Treatment*. New York: Basic Books, Inc., Publishers, 1961, revised 1977.

Rubin, L., *Facts and Feelings in the Classroom*. New York: Viking Press, 1973.

Sapir, Selma, and Bernice Wilson, *A Professional Guide to Working with the Learning Disabled Child*. New York: Brunner/Mazel, Inc., 1978.

Slingerland, Beth, *A Multi-Sensory Approach to Language Arts*. Cambridge, Mass.: Educators Publishing Service, Inc., 1978.

Weber, G. *Inner City Children Can Be Taught to Read—Four Successful Schools*. Washington, D.C.: Council for Basic Education, 1971.

Wiig, Elisabeth H., and Eleanor Messing Semel, *Language Dis-*

abilities in Children and Adolescents. Columbus, Ohio: Charles E. Merrill Publishing Co., 1976.

Pamphlets and Journals

Academic Therapy. 1543 Fifth Avenue, San Rafael, Ca. 94901.

Journal of Learning Disabilities. Professional Press, 5 N. Wabash Avenue, Chicago, Ill. 60602.

Learning Disability Quarterly. Dr. Donald D. Deshler, Department of Special Education, 435 Herbert C. Miller Building, University of Kansas Medical Center, 49th and Rainbow Blvd., Kansas City, Kan. 66103.

The Orton Society. 8415 Bellona Lane, Towson, Md. 21204. Bulletin and papers dealing with a wide variety of topics on learning disabilities are available through the Orton Society. A few samples: *Language Disabilities in Men of Eminence; Language Therapy to Salvage College Talents of Dyslexic Adolescents; The Language Continuum.*

The Reading Teacher. International Reading Association, 800 Barksdale Road, P.O. Box 8139, Newark, Delaware 19711. The International Reading Association also publishes books and pamphlets on many subjects concerning reading. A few samples: *Developing Study Skills in Secondary Schools*, Harold L. Herber; *Easy Reading: Book Series and Periodicals For Less Able Readers*, Michael Graves, Judith Boettcher, and Randall Ryder; *Using Sports and Physical Education to Strengthen Reading Skills*, Lance M. Gentile.

INDEX

371.92
Y 75

114 917